Winning the War for the Wealthy

How Life Insurance Companies Can
Dominate the Upscale Markets

by Russ Alan Prince

Winning the War for the Wealthy: How Life Insurance Companies Can Dominate the Upscale Markets

Russ Alan Prince

HNW Press

Printed in the United States of America. Printing number 1

ISBN number 0-9658391-2-5

Book design by: LUNA Corporate Design
Tel. 203-378-2543 • Email: LunaCorp@aol.com

Cover illustration: ©Elisabeth A. Lyon, Draw Me a Sheep Studios
Tel. 415-282-2825 • Email: blyon@sirius.com

Case writer: Lisa Novick • Email: LNovick@usc.edu

Other books by the author...

Published by HNW Press (203-255-8772)
- **The Perfect Legacy** ©1998

- **Building Your Business: Marketing Your Way to a $100 Million Investment Advisory Business** ©1997

Published by Lexington House (800-356-5936)
- **The Charitable Estate Planning Process: How to Find and Work with the Philanthropic Affluent** ©1994

- **Who's Afraid of Banks? Why Agents Need Not Fear Banks Selling Life Insurance** ©1997; booklet

Published by National Underwriter (800-543-0874)
- **The Charitable Giving Handbook** ©1997

- **Marketing to the Affluent: A Toolkit for Life Insurance Professionals** ©1995

- **Marketing to Family Business Owners: A Toolkit for Life Insurance Professionals** ©1995

- **Marketing Through Advisors: A Toolkit for Life Insurance Professionals** ©1996

- **Building an Affluent Clientele: Marketing Personal Lines to the Wealthy** ©1996

Published by Institutional Investor (212-224-3800)
- **Cultivating the Affluent II: Leveraging High-Net-Worth Client and Advisor Relationships** ©1997

- **Cultivating the Affluent: How to Segment and Service the High-Net-Worth Market** ©1995

Published by Jossey-Bass (888-378-2537)
- **The Seven Faces of Philanthropy** ©1994

Published by PMIC (800-633-7467)
- **Physician Financial Planning in a Changing Environment** ©1996

About the Author

Russ Alan Prince is President of Prince & Associates LLC, the leading strategy consulting and market research firm dedicated to the upscale markets.

Mr. Prince is a columnist for National Underwriter, Financial Planning Magazine and On Wall Street. He is also on the editorial board of Probe where his work appears regularly. Mr. Prince's comments have been reported in the Wall Street Journal, Barrons, Fortune, Forbes, BusinessWeek as well as numerous other national media.

Prince & Associates LLC works extensively with elite producers and those fast-tracking to elite status. The firm also works with selected forward-thinking financial institutions on strategy development and implementation.

Prince & Associates LLC
P.O. Box 843
Shelton CT 06484
203-924-5804

For

Sandi

- Russ Alan Prince

VI

Table of Contents

Appendices

Forward

Peter Drucker has said that "significant competitive advantage lies with those organizations and individuals who anticipate well in turbulent times." The financial services industry is indeed in the midst of turbulent times. Industry participants must swiftly confront and adapt to a competitive environment driven by deregulation, technological advancements and consolidation. Insurance companies, in particular, are faced with intense competition for clients from nontraditional sources such as commercial banks and investment banking firms.

The dramatic changes confronting insurance carriers and other financial service institutions have also generated much concern on the part of insurance producers. Over the past several years, I have personally experienced and witnessed a gradual shift in the attitudes of insurance producers from a passing curiosity with trends in the financial services industry to intense anxiety and uncertainty over the future of the insurance industry. Concern for the problems and opportunities created by shifting market dynamics has percolated from casual sidebar discussions among the progressive minority, to the main platform programs at various industry meetings. This is particularly common at programs frequented by the top producers who work primarily with successful public and private businesses and affluent individuals.

This concern and excitement resulting from such rapid change has led to the formation of Highland Capital Holding Corporation to take advantage of the new opportunities available to producers in the upscale markets. As part of the business development process, I sought out others with a shared vision for the potential opportunities created by the turbulent times facing the insurance industry. A well-known industry leader forwarded a copy of an article written by Russ Alan Prince. I was immediately impressed with Russ' abilities to capture and describe the fundamental changes affecting various members of the financial services industry, support his observations with objective research data, and offer creative and practical advice to industry participants seeking to capitalize on the systemic changes sweeping the industry.

Everyone is writing about and discussing change. No one, however, writes and speaks with more authority on the subject of change in the financial services industry that Russ Alan Prince. In *Winning the War for the Wealthy*, Russ not only forcefully describes the factors behind and the probable impact of the changing environment on both insurance companies and producers, but also suggests a prescription for success for those carriers and producers bold enough to take advantage of the resulting opportunities.

Russ understands the fears that plague (or should plague!) senior insurance executives and has his finger on the quickening pulse of top producers, accurately portraying their anxiety and concern. *Winning the War for the Wealthy* makes a compelling argument that *the* way for life insurance companies to dominate the upscale markets is through establishing true *partnerships* with elite producers that are best positioned as the advisors of choice for clients in the upscale markets.

I have personally benefited from Russ' unique ability to identify and articulate trends in the financial services industry as well as his sage observations regarding the resulting long term implications and opportunities. In many respects, the research data and opinions expressed in *Winning the War for the Wealthy* have mirrored the observations behind our own efforts in forming, together with several top producers, Highland Capital to create a home for those elite producer firms that desire to capitalize on the opportunities that Russ describes. I have listened carefully to Russ' sage observations and carefully considered the excellent empirical data generated by Prince & Associated LLC over the past several years. I encourage you to do the same as we together confront the turbulent times and resulting opportunities in the financial services industry of the 21st century.

John L. Robinson, Jr.
President and CEO
Highland Capital Holding Corporation

Strategic Leadership

UNDERSTANDING THE TERRAIN

"Read and reread the campaigns of Alexander, Hannibal, Ceasar,
Gustavus Adolphus, Turenne, Eugene and Fredrick.
Make them your models. This is the way to become a great captain
and to master the secrets of the art of war."
- Napoleon Bonaparte

"See the land, what it is: and the people that dwelleth therein,
whether they be strong or weak, few or many."
- Numbers 13:18

As a senior officer of an insurance company, you are faced with an array of issues that you need to address. You know that not addressing these issues is likely to result in the slow demise of your insurance company.

Just consider the following questions:

- Should you build up the career distribution system or discard it completely?
- Is an internal producer group the right way to go?
- Will a state-of-the-art investment advisory service put your company at a competitive advantage?
- How important are sophisticated case design support systems to your company?
- What distribution channels should you be using?
- How can you enhance the success of your wholesalers?
- How important are developing top producer exit strategies?

It is a truism to say that the insurance industry is changing. In fact, it is not only the insurance industry that is in turmoil; it is the entire financial services industry. By understanding the factors at play and by knowing your options, you can make informed strategic decisions.

To understand the importance of key factors that are impacting corporate strategy, we surveyed 182 members of insurance company senior management teams - Executive Vice Presidents, Presidents, Chief Executive Officers and Chairmen. Each survey participant represented a different life insurance company. Some of the companies in the study distribute exclusively through a career agency system, some rely exclusively on brokerage, and some were a hybrid of the two.

In making strategic decisions, you need to understand the terrain. The three key factors shaping the insurance industry terrain are:

• Dealing with the increasing complexity of competing in the financial services industry.
• The importance of the upscale markets.
• The dominant role of distribution.

Dealing with the Increasing Complexity of Competing in the Financial Services Industry

As noted above, the insurance industry is changing. It is a much more complex world. Nearly all insurance company top executives (97.3%) agree that dealing with industry complexity is of paramount strategic importance (see Exhibit 1.1).

The Core Responsibilities of Senior Management

The responsibility of dealing with industry complexity falls on the shoulders of senior management (see Exhibit 1.2). Leadership is essential. Nearly all the senior managers (98.9%) report that the quality of an insurance company's leadership will be the determining factor in insurance company success. Unfortunately, leadership is not always present (see Chapter 2).

There is also a shared awareness of the importance of being proactive in shaping the future. Most top insurance industry executives (73.6%) say that insurance companies need to be strategically proactive. Instead of responding to changing environmental scenarios and playing catch up, insurance companies must take the lead in creating the future of the financial services industry (see Chapter 3).

Exhibit 1.1 Dealing with Complexity

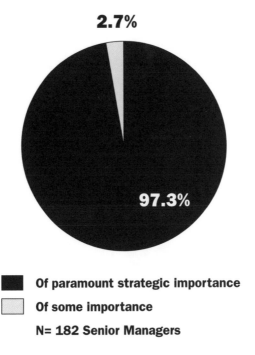

2.7%

97.3%

■ **Of paramount strategic importance**

□ **Of some importance**

N= 182 Senior Managers

The Use of Strategy Consultants

To meet their responsibilities, top management often relies on consultants. Consultants enable executives to better understand the financial services environment and to compete effectively. Most of the insurance companies in the study (92.3%) turn to strategy consultants (see Exhibit 1.3). It is worth noting that about half (46.4%) are dissatisfied with the experience (see Exhibit 1.4).

When carefully selected and managed, strategy consultants can be extraordinarily valuable. On the other hand, when they get "out of control" strategy consultants become a disappointment and an obstacle to success. In Appendix C, we discuss how to get the most from your strategy consultants.

Exhibit 1.2 The Core Responsibilities of Senior Management

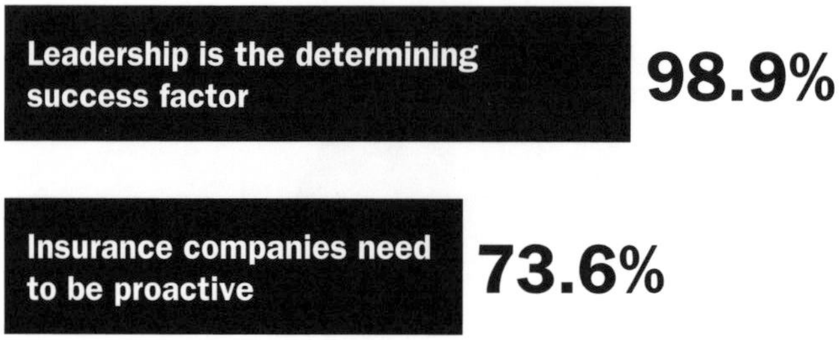

Leadership is the determining success factor **98.9%**

Insurance companies need to be proactive **73.6%**

N=182 Senior Managers

Exhibit 1.3 Have Employed Strategy Consultants

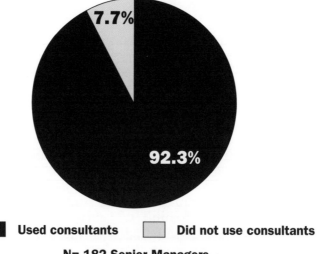

7.7%

92.3%

■ **Used consultants**   □ **Did not use consultants**

N= 182 Senior Managers

The Importance of the Upscale Markets

Our focus is on the upscale markets — privately held businesses and high-net-worth families. The upscale markets prove to be the place where the greatest leverage is possible. It is also the place where there is the greatest growth both in the United States and the world over.

Over the fifteen years we have been researching the financial and philanthropic behavior of the wealthy, we have found that they are the most risk-adjusted profitable segment for producers and all manner of financial institutions. Most financial institutions agree with this assessment; just look at the growth in competition for this segment.

Exhibit 1.4 Dissatisfied with the Experience

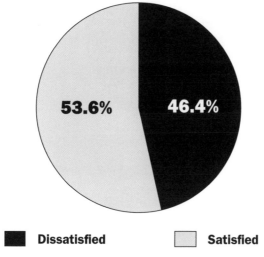

■ **Dissatisfied**   ☐ **Satisfied**

N= 168 Senior Managers

The value of upscale clients has not been lost on the insurance companies. Eight out of ten executives (80.2%) believe that upscale clients are extremely important to their insurance companies (see Exhibit 1.5).

High-net-worth clients are so attractive because they represent a good investment of resources, they often have business interests that open up cross-selling opportunities and they can refer other clients. Targeting upscale clients enables insurance companies to leverage their products, processes and technology.

Although upscale clients are strategically important to many insurance companies, we find insurance companies often fail to customize their approaches and tools to these markets. As the upscale markets will be the decisive battleground for quite a number of insurance companies, we discuss the most effective ways to segment (see Part II - Chapters 4 & 5) them.

Exhibit 1.5 The Importance of Upscale Clients

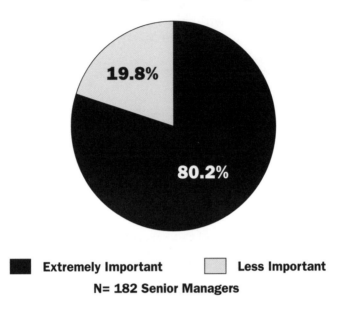

■ **Extremely Important**   ☐ **Less Important**

N= 182 Senior Managers

The Dominant Role of Distribution

With our focus on high-net-worth families and successful businesses, a critical consideration is how to most effectively market to them. In other words, what are the best ways to distribute insurance and investment products to the upscale markets?

At both strategic and tactical levels, 95.6% of the senior managers think that effective distribution would be one of the most important factors for insurance company success (see Exhibit 1.6). In fact, as part of the consolidation in the financial services industry, we will see more and more insurance companies investing in distribution systems. Just consider all the once independent broker/dealers insurance companies have been acquiring them at an ever accelerating pace.

The Need for Elite Producers

As distribution becomes all the more critical for developing upscale markets, most executives (87.4%) readily conclude that high-end producers are essential to work in the upscale markets (see Exhibit 1.7).

Exhibit 1.6 The Role of Distribution

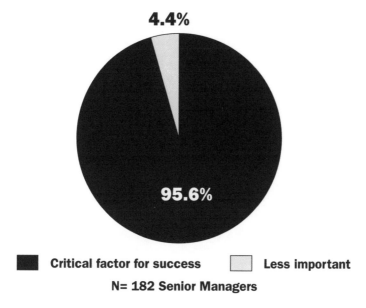

4.4%

95.6%

■ **Critical factor for success**   ☐ **Less important**

N= 182 Senior Managers

If insurance companies are going to capitalize on the potential of the upscale markets, they will need high-end producers to market their products. The best of these high-end producers we refer to as *elite producers.*

Exhibit 1.7 The Need for High-End Producers

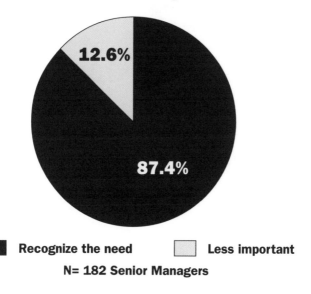

12.6%

87.4%

■ **Recognize the need**   ☐ **Less important**

N= 182 Senior Managers

Industry dynamics are changing for elite producers. They are becoming more and more aware of their importance to insurance companies. Moreover, when an insurance company works with elite producers the multiplier effect kicks in (see Chapter 7). Because of the decisive role played by elite producers, we devote Parts III, IV and V to exploring their world and how it is changing.

Winning a Producer's Business

Elite producers are becoming less loyal to insurance companies. This trend is not lost on insurance company executives. Most senior managers (88.5%) acknowledge that this is happening. Further, most of the senior managers (83.0%) understand that insurance companies are going to have to add more value if they want to win a producer's — especially an elite producer's — business (see Exhibit 1.8).

Insurance companies can win business in a number of ways. First and foremost, they need to have high-quality products and the requisite support. Even the "best" products are not enough, however. The insurance companies that will win the war for the wealthy will need to add value beyond quality products.

Based on extensive quantitative and qualitative research, we have identified key ways insurance companies can add value and win an elite producer's business (see Exhibit 1.9).

Exhibit 1.8 Changing Producer Loyalty

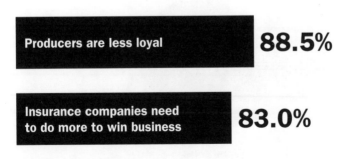

Producers are less loyal — **88.5%**

Insurance companies need to do more to win business — **83.0%**

N=182 Senior Managers

Exhibit 1.9   Ways Insurance Companies Can Add Value

Strategy	Discussed in
Strengthen the career agency system	Chapter 13
Establish internal producer groups	Chapter 14
Build a state-of-the-art investment advisory service	Chapter 15
Build a sophisticated case design support system	Chapter 16
Develop value-added wholesaling programs	Chapter 18
Develop top producer exit strategies	Chapter 19

Additional Distribution Systems

To dominate the upscale markets, elite producers are essential. However, not all elite producers are characteristic life insurance professionals. Most senior managers (76.9%) understand that they will need to work through a number of distribution systems aside from "agents" (see Exhibit 1.10). In Chapter 17, we discuss the potential of various distribution systems with respect to the upscale markets.

Exhibit 1.10 The Need for Additional Distribution Systems

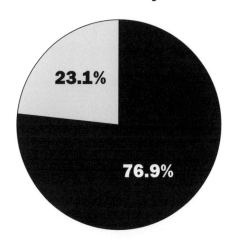

23.1%

76.9%

■ Additional distribution systems required

□ Current systems sufficient

N= 182 Senior Managers

The Bottom Line

Top insurance company executives have agreed. The fundamentals of the industry are changing, and willing insurance companies must change to survive. The broad outline of a successful strategy is also apparent. It involves the building blocks of focusing on the upscale markets, enlisting elite producers as strategic allies in the process, adding significant value for both clients and producers and exerting effective leadership. These are the topics of this book.

LEADING THE CHARGE

---

*"In war we must always leave room for strokes of fortune,
and accidents that cannot be foreseen."*
- Polybius

*"Be audacious and cunning in your plans, firm and persevering in
their execution, determined to find a glorious end."*
- Karl von Clausewitz

A peacetime army can perform adequately with decent management; leadership is an advantage, but not a necessity. In war, however, an army requires more than decent management. An army requires leadership in order to prevail.

The insurance industry, and the entire financial services industry, can be thought of as being at war. The opposing armies are the numerous financial services institutions. Victory is defined as the ability to succeed in such a highly competitive environment.

With dramatic changes impacting the financial services industry, the quality of the leadership will determine whether an insurance company will be triumphant in the war for clients. The quality of the leadership provided from the CEO and the senior officers of the carrier will affect every aspect of the insurance company. The carrier's fate, and that of all its stakeholders, rides on the shoulders of senior management.

The CEO and senior officers will have to deal with environmental as well as organizational changes. In terms of environmental changes, they will have to adjust swiftly and surely to competitive movement, deregulation, the changing nature of markets, the impact of advancing technology and more. In terms of organizational changes, senior management must deal with product diversification, industry consolidation, internal expansion, utilization of technology and the changing power dynamics of the distribution system.

This is a tall order. For some, it might seem overwhelming. Still, insurance companies can be innovative, entrepreneurial and aggressive in ways that will set the standard for the financial services industry. This standard will be due to the leadership abilities of the CEO and the senior officers.

Unfortunately, research indicates that only about 15 percent of senior insurance company management have these leadership qualities. While some insurance company CEOs are leading the charge, too many are biding their time — and may be managing their companies to defeat. In this economic era, insurance companies that are managed, not led, will be merged out of existence or acquired.

Creative Leadership

To be dominant in the financial services industry, CEOs and senior officers must be creative leaders. In the context of a large organization, such as an insurance company, this means that senior management must be able to do two things:

1. Create an agenda for advancement, and
2. Implement that agenda.

Creating the Agenda

The agenda hinges on the CEO's vision for the insurance company. Some CEOs want to create a full-service financial services firm; they want to be able to provide nearly every conceivable financial product and service to all major markets. Other CEOs are looking to solidify their position as a top-of-the-line insurance company offering premium products; although some other services and products might be a part of the overall mix, they will be a secondary focus. Yet another group of CEOs is focusing on markets to be served (middle market or upscale markets). Still others are seizing competitive advantage by focusing on distribution systems.

The logic of the vision is key. The vision must fit the immediate and long-term interests of all the stakeholders of the insurance company. The vision must also show an understanding of and willingness to influence the future.

Too often, blurry vision and reactive strategy are the norm. CEOs and senior officers often ignore the massive industry changes or play catch up instead of leading creatively.

Implementing the Agenda

Implementation is difficult. Yes, creating the agenda is an arduous and trying task: all assumptions need to be questioned, extensive empirical analysis is required and an honest assessment of the organization is essential. Nevertheless, this is simple in comparison to implementing the agenda.

Implementation needs a core group of highly dedicated and motivated individuals to drive the process. Networks of supportive relationships (both internal and external to the insurance company) are necessary in order to implement the strategy.

The process presents the greatest challenges and the greatest rewards. From the perspective of the insurance company, the focus should be on improving the operation, improving their position in the industry and improving the bottom line.

Leadership Qualities

Leading CEOs of the life insurance industry share nine qualities. These qualities play out in the setting and implementation of strategic agendas. CEOs and senior officers who share these leadership qualities will be able to take their insurance companies into the next millennium. The nine leadership qualities are:

1. Industry expertise.
2. Organizational skills and knowledge.
3. Strong industry relationships.
4. Excellent reputation.
5. The ability to think strategically and multidimensionally.
6. Exceptional interpersonal skills.
7. Integrity.
8. High energy levels.
9. Self-confidence.

Industry Expertise

All senior officers need to understand the nature of their companies. More and more, these companies are in the financial services industry, not just the insurance industry.

A CEO's industry expertise cannot possibly be comprehensive. However, it should be broadly based. Moreover, the CEO should have his own area of specialization, such as finance, operations or marketing. The same is true for the other senior officers.

During a time of rapid change, it can be a mistake to bring in a financial services industry outsider to be CEO. Leading at the top is not the same across all industries. For times as turbulent as these, the best CEOs and senior officers have an intimate knowledge of the dynamics and structure of the financial services industry.

Organizational Skills and Knowledge

The CEO and senior officers must coordinate resources within an organizational setting. Organizational skills and knowledge are critical in order to get things done.

The CEO and senior officers must be astute bureaucratic politicians. They must be able to weave alliances within the insurance company and be willing to let go of structures and processes that no longer serve the company well.

Strong Industry Relationships

The leadership must be well connected with other leaders in the financial services industry. With the changing structural environment, it is imperative that senior officers create ties with other financial institutions.

More than any time in the past, strategic alliances and consolidation are becoming the norm. Thus, the ability to find the best partners is essential. This requires strong industry relationships.

Excellent Reputation

Respect is a requirement of leadership. The reputation and accomplishments of the CEO and senior officers are of paramount importance. An effective way to win the respect of others is for the

CEO or senior officers to have proven themselves; others will scrutinize their track record, and be convinced.

Capability to Think Strategically and Multidimensionally

The financial services world is amazingly complex. There are no straightforward paths.

To be effective, CEOs and senior officers must think strategically and multidimensionally. They must think out-of-the-box. As in chess, they must also think quite a few moves ahead. They must look out into the future and see what is on the horizon in order to prepare for the forthcoming changes in their industry. Better yet, they must conceptualize and then work to create the future that will best work for them and for their company.

Exceptional Interpersonal Skills

CEOs and senior officers must work through other people to make things happen. They must motivate those who work for them and build strategic alliances among their peers. All these efforts require exceptional interpersonal skills. CEOs and senior officers need to be able to effectively communicate their vision and their commitment and transfer that passion to peers and subordinates.

Integrity

Honesty, veracity and probity are all signs of a principled creative leader. In the long run, others must have faith in the CEO's word. Integrity is essential.

High Energy Levels

Being the CEO or a senior officer of an insurance company is quite demanding. It requires that these professionals have a very high energy level in order to make things happen. Also, a high energy level is contagious and very motivating.

Self-Confidence

Leadership, by definition, requires people who are sure about themselves and their abilities. Being able to lead necessitates being self-assured. Even if a decision does not work out, leaders are not stopped — they continue on.

A leader cannot second-guess him or herself all the time. At the upper levels of management, a strong belief in the chosen strategy and tactics is essential.

Leading the Charge

The nine leadership qualities in Exhibit 2.1 are important to varying degrees based on the focus of the CEO and senior officers. Still, all of these qualities will be necessary for the CEO and senior officers to make the insurance company a significant long-term presence in the financial services industry.

Exhibit 2.1 The Importance of Selected Leadership Qualities to Creative Leadership

Leadership Qualities	Creating the Agenda	Implementing the Agenda
Industry expertise	High	Medium
Organizational skills and knowledge	Medium	High
Strong industry relationships	Low	High
Excellent reputation	Low	High
The ability to think strategically and mulitdimesionally	High	Medium
Exceptional interpersonal skills	Medium	High
Integrity	Medium	High
High energy levels	High	High
Self-confidence	High	High

Because of the complexity of the financial services industry, creating an intelligent agenda requires a tremendous amount of information and knowledge about finances, products, markets and the like. Thus, industry expertise is crucial in creating the agenda.

At the same time, the ability to think strategically and multidimensionally is also critical. A keen mind is paramount to take the mass of information and synthesize it into an actionable, viable agenda. Great vision is the product of a hard-working CEO and dedicated senior officers all drawing on the requisite expertise available. Great vision also entails being sure that the thought and analysis that developed the agenda are accurate.

To make the vision a reality, it is critical to attract, maintain and manage a large network of resources. This feat requires tremendous credibility. Therefore, the CEO and senior officers must have excellent reputations and must be perceived as possessing considerable integrity.

Organizational skills and knowledge come into play. Senior management must be able to get things done within the structure of the insurance company. They must also be able to reach out beyond their own firm to other firms in the financial services industry. They must have strong industry relationships.

Without exceptional interpersonal skills, the CEO and senior officers cannot make things happen. As implementation is the goal, the ability to work with and through people is acute. Tied to this are high energy levels as well as considerable self-confidence.

The Bottom Line

Looking down the road, we see that because of leadership most insurance companies will probably not last in their present form. Many will be merged or acquired in order for some of the value they have to survive.

The very best CEOs and senior officers — those with leadership qualities — are leading the charge into the 21st century both *for* their stakeholders and *against* their competitors.

CREATING THE FUTURE

"For great aims we must dare great things."
- Karl von Clausewitz

"In the art of war there are no fixed rules.
These can only be worked out according to the circumstances."
- Li Chuan

Strategic leadership is the art of the long-term view. A standard strategic leadership exercise is to compare the life insurance industry to other industries. Interesting observations emerge: Life insurance professionals are, without question, some of the most innovative and forward-thinking people in business. These professionals apply their creativity to developing and bringing new value-added products to market. All too often, however, these professionals are not applying this same entrepreneurial spirit to the strategic management of their insurance companies. The talent is there; it is simply a matter of using it.

An "installed base of thinking" — thinking that is out-of-touch with what is happening in the trenches — prevents insurance companies from dominating the financial services industry. Senior managers stick with formulas that were successful in the past, but do not spend enough time learning what would be successful today.

Some of the people running today's insurance companies alienate or isolate themselves in the stratosphere of "senior management" instead of being out with producers and clients. Moreover, these senior managers are harmfully distracted by the company's internal issues. Many senior managers are more involved with putting out fires than ascertaining what they need to do to be competitive next year, or five or ten years down the line. Political infighting often diverts resources and ideas into a black hole. As a result, few senior managers are sharply focused on working the trends and being strategic leaders. Few companies have a dynamic, shared vision of how the insurance company is going to be a major player in the financial services industry.

Insurance companies need to strategically plan and manage in the broad context of the financial services industry. Insurance companies are no longer simply competing among themselves; the battleground includes all the various financial services firms, from mutual fund complexes to banks and wirehouses, and even technology companies such as Microsoft.

In this cutthroat financial services environment, few insurance companies can plausibly identify themselves as standard bearers. By and large, other industries and companies are setting the agenda.

It is difficult to name an insurance company that is setting new rules for competition in the insurance industry, let alone the financial services industry. It is even more difficult to name an insurance company that is reshaping the very way business is conducted. And perhaps most difficult of all, is it possible to name any insurance companies that are deploying new capabilities that will transform the financial services industry?

Although there are notable exceptions, insurance companies are, for the most part, content to follow the status quo. Insurance companies follow the rules — rules set by *other firms* that are pushing the envelope. It is time for insurance companies to chart their own destiny and shape the financial services industry in their own interest.

The Need to Lead

Many insurance companies have restructured their operations. They have sought to extract the waste and become more profitable. This has proven largely effective.

Restructuring has helped to make insurance companies more viable. Previously, there was a great deal of waste. In many cases, the infrastructure had been created without concern for costs and was supported by the profitability of the sale of whole life insurance. With the shift in products, carriers needed to rationalize their expenses. Rarely, though, has restructuring ever resulted in fundamental improvements in the business. It is only a stop-gap measure, but one that often needs to be taken.

Insurance companies are more profitable when they are restructured. However, restructuring is not strategic leadership. Strategic leadership creates profits for tomorrow by delivering value though evolving lines of business, channels of distribution and clients. Only with strategic leadership can insurance companies create a highly rewarding future for themselves.

Many senior managers at many insurance companies focus their strategic planning efforts on the past and, sometimes, the present. These managers concentrate their energies and resources on understanding who their *current* clients are, what are the best distribution systems to reach these clients, who competes with the company for these clients, their strengths and weaknesses, their sustainable competitive advantages and their array of products. Although this analysis is indeed critically important, it is absolutely insufficient.

It is not enough to understand the competitive battleground today. It is equally, and in many situations, more important to understand the competitive battleground of tomorrow. Market leaders who fail to grasp the changing dynamics of their industry, and who fail to influence and adapt to those changes, will fail to be market leaders in the future.

Taking Charge

For insurance companies to be leaders, they must take charge of the process of industry transformation. To accomplish this, an insurance company must "reinvent" not only itself, but a significant component of the industry in which it operates. To accomplish this, an insurance company must develop and implement a strategy that catches the crest of the wave. It must position itself just ahead of dynamic changes that are transforming the financial services industry.

How are insurance companies to transform the financial services industry? They must create the future by taking command of emerging opportunities. Insurance companies can do this in a number of ways.

One approach is to change the way they compete. Another approach is to integrate aspects of other industries into their own, thus changing the competitive landscape. A third approach is to produce a variation on a set of services or products, and create a substantial new field as a result. This third approach is the most difficult but is also the most influential. It is also the way insurance companies can be most effective most quickly. A service and/or product focus is the strong suit of insurance companies. It is the way they have periodically been the leaders, the creators, of the financial services industry.

In the future, and even today, it will not be enough to merely develop the most advanced products and services. An integral and often disregarded aspect of this approach that will make the difference between success and failure is the ability to effectively distribute these products and/or services. Therefore, it is going to be essential to build an effective marketing front-end in order to reach the products or services potential profitability (see Appendix B).

Strategic Leadership

Strategy is the process of being victorious on the battleground of today's financial services industry. However, strategy is also determining who decides the battleground of tomorrow.

Strategic leadership is the culmination of three types of leadership:

- Intellectual Leadership.
- Structural Implementation Leadership.
- Market Share Leadership.

Intellectual Leadership

This is the first and an extremely critical step to success. It is essential to begin with a detailed understanding of prospective clients. Quite often, this is the place where many insurance carriers stumble. A detailed understanding of prospective clients extends far beyond basic demographics to a much more sophisticated level predicated on personality. High-net-worth psychology is critical for success in upscale markets (see Chapter 5).

Insurance companies need to understand who their clients are today, as well as who they will be in the near- and long-term. Remember, current and near-term clients are not necessarily the same.

In addition to a thorough grounding in current and prospective client behaviors, the insurance company must understand all the major trends impacting the financial services industry. These include demographic shifts, changing technologies and changes in the regulatory environment.

All told, intellectual leadership provides a perception of the future that incorporates the capabilities of the firm, the benefits it offers clients and the way to provide those benefits. In total, this is the insurance company's "vision."

A central aspect of intellectual leadership is the identification of "core competencies." These are bundles of skills, expertise and technology that result in particular benefits being provided to clients.

Leadership in a number of core competencies is the way an insurance company can exploit emerging opportunities and differentiate itself from competitors. The insurance company should benchmark itself against competitors to get a realistic picture of the uniqueness of its core competencies. In creating their future, most insurance companies should plan on augmenting their core competencies.

In order to create leverage, it is likely that insurance companies will establish strategic alliances with other financial institutions. For example, if an insurance company's core competencies include products, support services and the appropriate distribution system for corporate benefit cases, it can establish a strategic alliance with another insurance company to obtain Section 125 services and provide them through its distribution channels. Each of the companies would be leveraging different core competencies; one is leveraging its distribution system, and the other is leveraging its product expertise.

The best way to develop a position of intellectual leadership is through scenario building. This entails using different sets of assumptions to construct various future scenarios. With respect to developing and creating action plans around likely future scenarios, stochastic modeling should be employed.

Structural Implementation Leadership

Using the insights gained in constructing future scenarios, insurance companies can act to influence the direction of the financial services industry. At this stage, the insurance company utilizes existing core competencies and obtains additional core competencies that will enable it to create the future.

Senior management must establish the strategic architecture. This is the high-level blueprint for actualizing the chosen scenario. In the strategic blueprint, the steps needed to create the desired future are spelled out.

In short, an insurance company must create new competitive advantages. It is useful to think of the insurance company as a portfolio of resources that needs to be optimized. Often it is necessary to go beyond existing resources to other portfolios of resources (i.e., other financial and professional services companies). These strategic alliances permit insurance companies to leverage their core competencies as well as those of other firms.

Marshaling resources is an entrepreneurial activity, and it is vital for the company to be able to take advantage of future trends. The entrepreneurial spirit must be a balance of business savvy and creative talent. This spirit, however, is all too often hampered by bureaucratic malaise.

Market Share Leadership

With the vision of the future clearly defined and the infra-structure in place, the insurance company must craft an appropriate marketing strategy to garner clients. At the same time, the insurance company must manage the competitive environment by preempting other financial services firms in critical markets.

First movers have the advantage in creating an installed base of clients. These clients tend not to be easily shifted. To usurp first movers requires significant investment in higher quality products, services and value-added.

It is equally important for the insurance company to create brand equity for its products, services, distribution system and firm. In an industry that is as commoditized as the financial services industry, brand equity will be valuable for obtaining clients and will help the insurance company develop a distinctive leadership role.

The Bottom Line

An insurance company can control its own destiny by influencing the destiny of the financial services industry. Insurance companies cannot be content with transforming only themselves. They must look outward and transform the financial services industry. The insurance industry already possesses the talent to do so; all that is necessary is the entrepreneurial will to act.

From producers to senior management, the abilities of many people in the insurance industry are unsurpassed. If these innovative individuals were not available, it would not be fair to criticize the insurance industry for failing to set the financial services agenda. But these individuals are available. These highly talented and resourceful life insurance specialists must be tapped, directed and focused so that they can create the future of the financial services industry.

Worlds
of
Wealth

II

SOURCES OF WEALTH

"Knowledge, if it does not determine action, is dead to us."
- Plotinus

"Time spent in reconnaissance is seldom wasted."
- British Army Field Service Regulations, 1912

For producers, the future is in the upscale markets. The upscale markets are growing faster and commanding disproportionately greater assets than the population at large. The upscale markets require complex financial services and products, and are willing and able to pay for them. Producers have their greatest leverage, and the greatest return for their efforts, in these markets.

The upscale markets are composed of high-net-worth individuals and families, and small- and mid-sized firms and professional practices. Often the high-net-worth individual makes decisions for his or her personal finances and for the enterprise(s) he or she owns. When considering opportunities in the high-net-worth market, producers must look at both the business side and the personal side of the equation.

How to Become Wealthy

One of the fastest ways of making it to the top of the financial ladder is to marry money. The only problem is that people who do this usually have money but no life. And in the end, the money usually is not theirs. People who marry money are, in effect, borrowing it as long as the relationship keeps on track. Some people have made their fortune by marrying right, but these people are the exceptions. They might have a wonderful marriage and the keys to the vault, but the more common scenario is less attractive. So much for marrying money.

There are other ways of becoming wealthy. The six types of wealth are:

- Equity wealth.
- Post-equity wealth.
- Salaried wealth.
- Inherited wealth.
- Illegal wealth.
- Fortuitous wealth.

Equity Wealth

Throughout the world, equity wealth is the most common route to affluence. This type of wealth results from owning an equity stake in a business that makes a great deal of money. Most of the time, such companies are family businesses.

Another version of equity wealth results from effort. There may be more millionaire insurance agents than any other type of high-end service provider. Frank, for example, is a veteran top producer who has become quite wealthy by catering to the wealthy. He has been at the job for more than thirty years. Frank is considered one of the equity wealthy because he has a personal stake in the business he generates.

Professional investors are also an example of the equity wealthy. Their decisions determine whether they will eat filet or ground round. A direct relationship exists between the fortunes of the equity wealthy and the prosperity of their enterprises.

Post-Equity Wealth

Paul is an example of post-equity wealth. Of the World War II generation, he spent more than forty years building up his business. Year after year, his family did without so that he could grow his company. And grow it did. From a firm that had three employees — himself, his brother and his wife — it grew to a company of approximately 350 employees. And when Paul sold his company, he became wealthy —very wealthy.

In the 1980s, large corporations rushed to buy smaller firms. During that time, Paul was approached about selling his family business. The money was too good to pass up. Paul was sure that he was being offered too much for his company, but he did not want to argue with the Wall Street professionals. He sold his equity in the firm and became quite well-to-do. His brother, spouse, and children, as well as a number of other senior employees of the firm, did the same.

Paul's family is an example of post-equity wealth. They became rich when they sold the enterprise that gave them their livelihood. Incidentally, Paul's company which has since become about 20 percent more profitable, was sold again in 1992 for nearly forty percent less than he, his family and key employees were paid for it.

Salaried Wealth

We sometimes read about Chief Executive Officers taking home millions in pay and bonuses. However, salaried wealth tends not to be the most likely way to make a fortune.

There are, of course, numerous high-income professions that make people financially secure, but few of these professions can make people wealthy. Physicians, or attorneys or accountants who accumulate great wealth are most likely partners in a practice; their moneys are not due to salaries but equity wealth.

Inherited Wealth

Goethe noted, "What you have inherited from your father, you must earn over and over again." Being born with the proverbial silver spoon in your mouth can sometimes end up being as much of a curse as a blessing.

"Trust babies" are people of all ages who are financially secure because someone along the way established a trust fund for them. The trust fund bestows financial freedom so that these people can direct their energies to do great things, nothing at all or something in between.

Although inherited wealth sometimes receives a lot of attention in the media, it accounts for a very small portion of the wealthy. Inherited wealth is also regularly tied up in trusts and by family advisors.

Illegal Wealth

As the Soviet Union was collapsing, an ex-KGB Colonel no more than five-feet-tall walked into a Swiss private bank. To his right and left were his two "nephews." Each nephew was more than six-feet six-inches tall. They were wearing trench coats that bulged slightly.

The ex-KGB Colonel and his nephews had been expected. They were ushered into a sound-proof private room where armed security professionals were waiting. Also present were the representatives of a rare-stone-purchasing consortium. The ex-KGB Colonel opened the briefcase he was carrying and meticulously emptied out its contents of white uncut diamonds. The representatives of the purchasing consortium assessed the value of the diamonds at approximately $50 million. The private bankers received a one percent fee for arranging everything, and currently manage the funds for the ex-KGB Colonel.

The ex-KGB Colonel explained that when things settle down in his homeland, he will go back and be a capitalist. No one bothered to tell him that he already was.

Illegal wealth is the largest type of wealth in the world, but has some drawbacks. Pablo Escobar, of Colombia, was worth trillions until he became the big loser in a confrontation with the law.

There are two basic types of illegal wealth:

- Criminal activities.
- Flight capital.

Criminal Activities

Drug traffickers, like the late Pablo Escobar, deal in enormous amounts of cash and must contend with foreign currency issues. The same is true of arms dealers, who are doing a booming business of late, and others like them.

These types of criminals are not the only ones dependent on financial secrecy to manage their affairs. All forms of criminal activity require the adroit management of the money trail. Mechanisms are needed for the money to be "cleaned."

Evading taxes, a criminal activity in the United States, is not a criminal activity in Switzerland. Swiss private bankers have a saying, "There would be no tax havens without tax hells." As taxes increase, so does the impetus to circumvent them.

Flight Capital

Political risk is the possibility of losing assets because of changing governmental controls. An affluent business owner, for example, may fear the confiscation of his or her property as a new political reform party comes to power. Political instability causes a deep distrust of visible assets because they can be easily appropriated.

Flight capital is triggered by existing or anticipated adverse changes in the political, economic and social environments of countries. It is impossible to know how much wealth is in flight. At best, the flow of moneys out of host countries can only be estimated by using broad economic measures of questionable accuracy. For example, more than $200 billion was estimated to have fled developing countries between 1976 and 1985. Of that sum, between 1983 and 1985, $50 billion was estimated to have left countries that were having difficulty servicing their national debt.

Estimations of flight capital are further complicated by an inability to determine what portion is due to criminal activities. In the numbers cited above, the extent to which those monies represent criminal activities is considered high, but impossible to establish.

Political risks stop at the border. This makes assets secretly held outside of the country all the more valuable. In many countries, such as those in South America, it is illegal to move money outside the country. Thus the need for financial secrecy.

I strongly advise, on moral grounds alone, to avoid anyone who has become wealthy through illegal means.

Fortuitous Wealth

When someone gets lucky and becomes rich, that is fortuitous wealth. This kind of wealth takes all the hard work and effort out of the process. A National Clearing House winner is a good example of someone with fortuitous wealth.

Consider Brazilian legislator Joao Alves. He has a fortune equivalent to $51 million U.S. He told a congressional panel investigating corruption that he had been on a winning streak. He claimed that he had amassed this wealth by winning the Brazilian national and local lotteries and national bingo. It had been an amazing winning streak. To accumulate that much money he'd have had to have won more than 24,000 times in five years. This is an example of either fortuitous or illegal wealth. The congressional panel has yet to decide.

Some would say that inherited wealth is fortuitous wealth, that being born is not a proactive means of becoming affluent. This is a good argument, but by most definitions, fortuitous wealth happens after a person has been around for a while.

Being lucky is not something to depend on, although a fair number of people seem to do just that. A lucky feeling when buying a lottery ticket slightly increases one's odds of winning a multi-million dollar lottery. Although this approach to becoming wealthy is one of the least demanding, it is also the most unpredictable and least likely to occur.

The Bottom Line

The most common way to become affluent is by having a piece of a successful enterprise — being equity wealthy. In fact, the other forms of wealth also tend to be based on having an equity stake somewhere along the way. Post-equity wealth works this way. Inherited wealth is also usually a result of equity wealth. Even illegal wealth is usually due to an equity position. Only salaried wealth and fortuitous wealth cannot be tied to equity wealth.

Directly or indirectly, most private wealth derives from business ownership. Understanding the sources of private wealth is essential when it comes to designing product and marketing strategies. This is why many producers who specialize in serving the needs of wealthy clients usually bring both personal and business expertise to bear.

HIGH-NET-WORTH PSYCHOLOGY

"If one knew the enemy's intentions beforehand one could always defeat him even with an inferior army."
- Frederick the Great

"The sinews of war are infinite money."
- Cicero

Although the source of wealth is telling and will be a key to determining which products and services to provide, high-net-worth psychology is the secret to success with the affluent. High-net-worth psychology means the underlying logic of how high-net-worth individuals select financial advisors, make financial decisions and develop long-term relationships. Understanding why the high-net-worth individual stays with key financial advisors is the answer to building a financially and personally rewarding practice in the most significant market today.

High-net-worth psychology is essential for producers and the financial institutions that support them. For producers, high-net-worth psychology makes prospecting, sales and client-retention efforts more effective and efficient. Knowing high-net-worth psychology enables producers to leverage their time and energies in order to significantly enhance their practices. By using high-net-worth psychology, producers achieve greater prospecting success, shorter closing cycles *and* better client retention. High-net-worth psychology enables producers to reach higher levels of productivity more quickly, and to stay there.

For insurance companies, high-net-worth psychology becomes essential in all R&D efforts, from product design and enhancement to developing producer support services. High-net-worth psychology is, or should be, a central component of the strategic planning and marketing of every insurance company targeting the upscale markets. Every producer working in the advanced markets and insurance company needs to understand high-net-worth psychology.

The Nine Profiles of Wealth

Elite producers instinctively use their personal formulations of high-net-worth psychology. Their psychological insights come from extensive personal experience and good instincts. In some insurance companies and other financial institutions, senior management has demonstrated that they, too, possess similar insight. Recent research has taken these insights and personal experiences and constructed a formal system of high-net-worth psychology.

High-net-worth psychology answers all the "why" questions. Why do the affluent switch financial advisors? Why do the affluent prefer certain products over others? Why do some affluent people have many advisors and some depend on just one? Why do the affluent select certain advisors and not others?

Based on more than ten years of quantitative and qualitative research, nine profiles of wealth have been identified. These are the nine types of high-net-worth psychology. Portions of this research have been published in *Private Asset Management* (Institutional Investor), one of the sponsors of the research. The nine profiles are:

- Family Stewards.
- Financial Phobics.
- Independents.
- The Anonymous.
- Moguls.
- VIPs.
- Accumulators.
- Gamblers.
- Innovators.

Family Stewards

Family Stewards is the most common profile of the affluent. One in five high-net-worth individuals are Family Stewards. Family Stewards' interests center on their family. They like to do a good job with their financial affairs, which usually entails selecting high-quality advisors, in order to take good care of their family. They are generally risk adverse.

Brian Grey is a Family Steward. Brian started as a food importer and then branched out into food production. Over the years, all of his children worked in the company, and his son is now being groomed to take over day-to-day company management.

Brian started working with Paul, his financial advisor, very early. His first concern was carrying enough insurance to protect his family. Over the years, Paul has installed a corporate benefits program for Brian, as well as continuing to handle his family's insurance and investment needs. Paul is currently working with Brian on succession planning issues and charitable giving.

This sort of close relationship between producer and Family Steward client is common. Although Family Stewards will also be close to their accountants and attorneys, financial advisors like insurance producers hold a unique place as an advisor because of the comprehensive support they can provide. Family Stewards are very loyal; they will not "shop" their business around, and they will generally trust their financial advisors to deliver whatever they say they can.

Financial Phobics

Financial Phobics are not interested in personally dealing with their financial affairs. They dislike being involved in investment decisions. They prefer, if not insist, that their financial advisors handle everything. They are also risk adverse, and often prefer traditional (i.e., safe) products.

Patricia Osman is a Financial Phobic. Her husband of 35 years just died, and she inherited everything. Her husband handled all the financial affairs of the family, and she feels lost, frustrated and overwhelmed. She is terribly afraid of making a mistake which could harm her children's inheritances, but is not motivated to learn about investments and financial affairs herself. It would be easy if she felt comfortable with her husband's financial advisor, but she doesn't. All he wanted to talk about were complicated things she did not understand.

At a widow's support group, she heard Mary talk about Larry, a financial advisor she was working with. Mary introduced Patricia to Larry, and they hit it off. Larry was interested in a lot of the things Patricia was interested in like travel and gardening, and he made complicated financial ideas simple and easy to understand.

Financial Phobics select advisors emotionally. They want to be able to trust someone else to take care of the complicated details and to make the wise choices. Once they make a selection, they are extremely loyal. They can be demanding, but it is because of their fear. They need personal contact and reassurance, not complicated analyses.

Independents

Independents are somewhat more involved in the process of managing their financial affairs. For them, making sure that their financial affairs are in order provides them a sense of financial freedom. Their financial advisors must help them set a clear path to follow, but need to appreciate that this segment is quite skeptical.

Fred Kovaks grew up during the '60s, and although he did not rebel, he did absorb a lot of the feelings of the times. He started a consulting company which has been quite successful in its niche. Fred is currently unhappy with Gary, his financial advisor. Gary just completed a retirement plan for Fred, but with all the wrong assumptions. Gary assumed Fred would want to stay in the company till about 65, while Fred dreamed of getting on his Harley and heading west. Like many Independents, Fred seeks financial success in order to buy personal freedom.

Independents are less loyal than other segments. They will switch advisors, including insurance agents, if they do not feel understood. They do not place much trust in others.

The Anonymous

The Anonymous are very concerned with confidentiality. They believe that secrecy about their financial concerns is important. In general, the Anonymous use very few advisors, and are the most loyal of all the psychological types.

Simon Grazier is one of the Anonymous. Betsy was able to pick this up when Simon asked that the door be closed before they started to talk. Later on, she discovered he was glad to see that she was a "clean-desk" type, who never left files and papers on view. In order to reassure Simon that all his affairs would be kept confidential, Betsy was careful to use registered mail or overnight services for documents, and to stamp other material "confidential."

Simon is typical for the Anonymous. Financial advisors working with this type need to be very reassuring about issues of privacy and confidentiality. In return, the Anonymous clients will be very loyal.

Moguls

Moguls are oriented toward achieving personal power. Through the skilled management of their financial affairs, they can exercise influence. Their advisors must be alert to issues of power and its uses when working with Moguls.

Fred McKinty is well known in the community. The owner of an oil heating company, he is very active in local politics. He is a financial supporter as well as board member of local charities and the community foundation. Fred likes to be known as someone "important to know," and relishes being in the center of things.

George is Fred's advisor, and George treats Fred well. Right now, George is working up a proposal for a private foundation for Fred, knowing that he will be attracted to the prestige and especially the power that goes along with a foundation.

Moguls like power and influence. They like to make things happen in their businesses and in their communities. Often they are able to be powerful because they have the resources, the money, to do so. Moguls can be profitable, if difficult and demanding, clients. They like to be catered to and need their power acknowledged. They can be very powerful allies in the search for new clients, as they know a lot of people.

VIPs

VIPs are focused on personal prestige issues. They tie their financial planning to matters of status and how well they are respected by other people. Financial advisors of VIPs must recognize this and respond accordingly.

Allison and George Martin are VIPs. They live in the best neighborhood and drive prestigious SUVs. Whenever anyone wants to know what the right thing to do or buy is, they call Allison because she always knows. She is active in the right charities; George sits on the board of a well chosen few.

Steve, their insurance and financial advisor, met them through their charity work. Steve has helped the Martins with some tax-advantaged charitable giving and worked with the charity to be sure their gift was properly appreciated with a ceremony, award dinner, press coverage and a plaque.

VIPs crave social recognition. They like the outward manifestations of success and prestige. They want to be recognized as important people. This need for status carries over into their financial decision-making. VIPs are eager to have the kind of investments the very wealthy have and are interested in investments and insurance with a cachet.

Accumulators

Accumulators are concerned with amassing wealth — first, last, always. They believe a person can never be too rich. Moreover, they will readily acknowledge their sole objective is to create, enhance and preserve their wealth. They seek financial advisors who understand their sole interest and can achieve high rates of return.

Joe March is an Accumulator. He owns an engineering firm and approaches investing with the same precision and eye for detail he applies to his company. Barry has been his advisor for years. Barry knows now to describe all financial options in terms of rate of return, and has been successful selling asset protection and tax-advantaged investment products on this basis.

Accumulators are good clients who have high rates of savings. They are a continual source of new funds to place under management or otherwise invest. Accumulators are excellent prospects for performance products. If they are getting the products they want from an advisor, they will stick; however, they are the first to leave if performance declines.

Gamblers

Gamblers relish the process of financial management. Gamblers, for instance, treat investing as a hobby. They derive pleasure from playing the markets. Because of their knowledge and risk profile, Gamblers are a challenge for advisors.

Frank Larson is a Gambler. He will move money into a product on impulse. He is an avid reader of financial reporting and thinks he is a savvier investor than he actually is. He is eager for the "quick kill," and will tend to focus on the one outstanding result rather than the overall pattern of return. Harold has been working with Frank long enough to know he has to boost his energy level when talking to Frank.

Gamblers are good clients for advisors who will invest the time to talk to them. Since financial management is their hobby, they consume large amounts of information because they always want to be "in the know" and not miss anything. Advisors who invest the time it takes to keep a Gambler happy will find a loyal client in return.

Innovators

Innovators like to be at the cutting edge of financial technology. That is, they are always aware of the latest financial services and products. Their advisors must themselves be state-of-the-art. Innovators will switch advisors if they sense that someone else is more tied into the latest thinking on insurance, investment and financial management issues.

Sal Munakata is an Innovator. Sal's specialty chemical company has been successful, and Sal's passion for being at the cutting edge has spilled over into his approach to personal financial management. Sal is more than willing to learn about complex products, since he believes that complexity will yield a better honed result. Lester has been working with Sal for some time and has learned to schedule a couple hours for their meetings, because Sal is eager to soak up all the information Lester can provide.

Innovators like to know that their decisions are consistent with the state-of-the-art in financial thinking and take advantage of the latest changes in tax regulations. Innovators are demanding in their own way, although advisors generally like to work with someone whose enthusiasm for the details of financial management equals theirs. Innovators will remain loyal to an advisor who keeps them at the cutting edge, but will often have several advisors so they can compare solutions.

Using High-Net-Worth Psychology

High-net-worth psychology is applicable to all aspects of marketing and working with affluent clients, from prospecting to relationship management. High-net-worth psychology enables the producer to focus prospecting efforts, to customize sales efforts and to develop long-term relationships with upscale clients.

Here is how prospects are "sold." Most insurance agents will begin by explaining what they do and how they do it. Prospective clients want to know how the producer's services and products will permit them to achieve *their* goals and objectives.

High-net-worth psychology now comes into play. It provides a framework through which the producer can communicate the benefits of his or her products and services. High-net-worth psychology positions those services and products. For instance, the prospect's financial personality defines how much technical detail a producer should reveal. For Innovators, internal rate of return and detailed financial comparisons are often appropriate. At the opposite pole, Financial Phobics are not interested in these issues at all and will be turned off if the subject is broached.

By using high-net-worth psychology in one-to-one situations, the producer creates a higher level of rapport more quickly. At the same time, the producer is able to do a better job by being able to identify and address his or her client's needs and wants. High-net-worth psychology is very effective at finding upscale clients as well as assisting in maintaining strong relationships with them.

High-net-worth psychology can also be used to produce effective handout materials that demonstrate why the particular insurance agent is the right financial advisor for the prospect. High-net-worth psychology has also been extensively employed in designing seminar programs that are about the attendees.

In relationship management, high-net-worth psychology is a framework that gives insurance producers insight into the nature and amount of interaction that they should have with their affluent clients. For instance, for optimal results with The Anonymous, meetings should be periodic (about five or six times a year) and the matter of confidentiality should be brought up by the producer at every meeting. At each of these meetings, the producer should explain that confidentiality is a very important aspect of their business and that he or she recognizes that it is very important to the client.

The Bottom Line

There is now considerable academic and applied empirical research on high-net-worth psychology. High-net-worth psychology has been shown to be core to the financial affairs of the wealthy, small- and mid-sized businesses and to professional practices, from life insurance and investments to fiduciary services and credit.

Of greater significance is the success producers have when they incorporate high-net-worth psychology into their prospecting, selling and relationship management activities. The use of high-net-worth psychology is critical in building an exceptionally successful financial advisory business.

Financial institutions are increasingly recognizing the power of high-net-worth psychology and are using the framework in their strategic and marketing initiatives. In such a competitive environment, the insights provided by high-net-worth psychology are crucial.

Elite Producers

ELITE PRODUCERS DOMINATE
THE UPSCALE MARKETS

*"Never fight against heavy odds if, by any possible maneuvering,
you can hurl your whole force on a part,
and that the weakest part, of your enemy and crush it."*
- Napoleon Bonaparte

"Always mystify, mislead and surprise the enemy."
- Stonewall Jackson

Talented insurance agents are the dominant financial professionals in the upscale markets. Other top financial and legal professionals also work with upscale clients, doing an exceptional job and prospering, but when they are compared to the very best producers from the insurance industry, the insurance agents dominate. Without question, there are sensational stockbrokers, attorneys, accountants and bankers, but the "best of the best" among these professionals are no match for the "best of the best" of the insurance industry.

This conclusion is based on more than a decade of empirical research on the upscale markets and the distribution systems of professional and financial services to these markets. There is no group of professionals more gifted, dedicated, client-focused and innovative than high-end insurance agents.

The Upscale Markets

To put this in perspective, when people in the financial services industry talk about the upscale markets, they are referring to the affluent and to successful businesses.

Who is considered affluent depends on who is providing the service. When investment management firms talk about the affluent, they are usually talking about people with $1 million or more in *liquid assets*. They estimate that there are 3.2 million such investors (with combined assets of $7.1 trillion) living in the United States.

When estate planning life insurance agents talk about the affluent, they are more likely referring to people with an *estate* of $5 million or more. The point is that the affluent have the need for and the resources to buy the products and services that financial and legal professionals provide.

Aside from the affluent, successful businesses are the other component comprised by the upscale market. Some of these businesses are Fortune 500 companies. However, the vast majority are smaller, usually family-owned firms. Family-owned businesses account for 90 percent of all the companies in the United States and half of the GDP.

When it comes to personal production (the providing of financial services), the upscale markets are the ones that provide meaningful leverage. They are where a producer can add value and where he or she is appropriately compensated for adding that value.

Reaching Top of the Table or the Chairman's Council of an insurance company requires working predominantly with the affluent and/or businesses because there is only so much time in a day. As a result, competition for these clients is quite keen; everyone in the financial services industry wants to work with them. It is the insurance agents, however, who prove to be the most adept at working in these worlds of wealth.

Three Reasons Why Insurance Agents Dominate

Three key attributes characterize high-end insurance agents and make them superior to all other competitors seeking to serve the affluent market. These attributes are:

- An entrepreneurial orientation.
- Technical expertise.
- Exceptional interpersonal skills.

These characteristics describe elite insurance producers, rarely the other providers of products and services to the upscale markets.

An Entrepreneurial Orientation

Many of the most creative, forward-thinking and goal-oriented people providing financial services have chosen to become life insurance professionals. They like the independence and the ample rewards for individual action. These producers are highly motivated to make things happen because their success depends on their own actions. This is why they are so often the first to innovate in financial services.

High-end insurance agents will be the winners as deregulation and market forces blur the lines between the various types of financial services. Although stockbrokers are beginning to feel their way into the insurance business by promoting estate planning and employee benefits, insurance agents are aggressively and very successfully entering the fee-based investment advisory business.

Many top-of-the-line stockbrokers will be successful at marketing insurance. However, their success will pale in comparison to the asset-gathering success of high-end insurance agents. For example, Robert, a member of a producer group, decided to expand his upscale practice into fee-based money management. He began by thinking through his options and his plans. Since he was already quite prosperous, he needed to think through whether he really wanted to put in the time and effort that would be required to make the shift. He also thought about his current client base to assess the opportunities for money management services. He decided that the potential was there and that he liked the idea of the challenge, so he moved to the next step.

He evaluated his resources. Entrepreneurs are successful because they are skilled at identifying and leveraging all the resources available to them. Robert conducted an industry survey and began to familiarize himself with the most important types of resources available — the hundreds of financial institutions, consultants and coaches all wanting to work with top producers to help them thrive as fee-based investment advisors. Robert quickly saw that he had to link up with the most promising resource system so that the business infrastructure would be in place for him to begin working with clients.

As it turned out, the broker/dealer used by his producer group provided the investment product line as well as the back-office systems he required. This made things relatively easy for him operationally. He then invested in the front-office technology.

As the operational side was falling into place, Robert decided to freshen up on the technical side of the investment management business, such as modern portfolio theory. He also needed to learn the specific demands of marketing fee-based investment advisory services because they differ significantly from the demands of marketing the insurance-based services in which he had specialized. He developed this expertise by going back to school on the technical matters, working with consultants and joining an advisor network (the investment advisory business equivalent of a study group) for the marketing expertise.

These steps took Robert about six months on a part-time basis. All the while, he continued to service his insurance clients. Because of his entrepreneurial approach, the investment advisory side of his business has taken off during the past three years.

From the time he decided to enter the fee-based investment advisory business, it took him about three years to bring nearly $100 million under management. The assets are split about 75 percent private clients and 25 percent retirement funds. On the private clients, he averages 80 basis points annually. For the retirement assets, he averages 35 basis points annually. In the forthcoming year, he will earn $687,500, presuming the asset base remains the same. This is in addition to his successful existing insurance practice. Because of the way Robert structured his investment advisory business, these monies will go to the bottom line and into his pocket.

By approaching the problem with an entrepreneurial attitude, Robert made the moves that paid off and created success, and he is far from an anomaly among high-end insurance agents moving into the fee-based investment advisory business. For these high-end insurance agents, providing fee-based investment advisory services turns out to be significantly easier than providing insurance services. More and more high-end insurance agents are making the move toward fee-based money management.

Technical Expertise

Strong technical skills are required to effectively work with the affluent and with business clients. The issues these clients face are complex. High-end insurance agents must bring to these clients an outstanding knowledge of the tax laws, accounting procedures, product knowledge and the trends in the financial services industry.

When working with upscale clients, life insurance professionals need to be part attorney, part accountant, part investment advisor, part private banker as well as total insurance professional. High-end insurance producers are more than up to the task.

Few high-end insurance producers are polymaths. Instead, they have their own niches of expertise and rely on associates to provide the specialized knowledge and skills they personally do not have. No other type of financial professional proactively builds and works with networks of other top-of-the-line legal and financial professionals as well as top insurance agents do.

For the most part, insurance agents are quite humble about their excellent technical skills. They are not looking for the limelight. Instead, they prefer to be recognized for their expertise and knowledge among their clients, peers and other professionals.

Barbara is an example of a high-end insurance agent who is a true financial wizard. Her clientele is primarily mid-sized businesses. She takes the role of a general contractor, bringing in and supervising the activities of her associates, the subcontractors. She is a one-woman-shop with four technical support people — three accountants and one attorney — and a clerical staff of three. She has an advanced business degree from Yale's School of Organization and Management.

She claims her success is her network of other insurance agents, accountants and attorneys who can answer any conceivable technical question. Moreover, she says she wins business by being the most erudite, the most technically adept professional discussing financial services with mid-sized business owners and their accountants.

When she has competition from financial or human resource consulting professionals, she knows that they are presenting "pretty basic ideas" to the business owner and his or her accountants. As a result, when she gets her turn, she dazzles the prospective client with her understanding of the various sophisticated courses of action that can be taken and her in-depth understanding of their business concerns. Part of her persuasiveness is her ability to tell stories of other similar cases she has handled successfully.

In addition to insurance products, Barbara is extensively involved in every aspect of benefits planning for her clients. This often extends to the design and implementation of current compensation systems.

Barbara outshines her competition because she is, indeed, more intelligent and more ingenious. She is also perpetually enhancing her technical skills and expanding her network of like-minded financial and legal professionals.

In one case, Barbara solved a business owner's problem by transferring the ownership of his business to his employees. She used a charitable remainder trust, where the remaindermen will create an endowed private foundation, a charitable lead trust and an employee stock ownership plan to make the transfer work in the most tax-efficient way possible. To put something like this together necessitates a very high level of technical facility as well as exceptional interpersonal skills to keep everyone on track and happy.

Barbara, like Robert, has expanded into the investment advisory business for high-net-worth executives and retirement plans. This will enhance her ability to provide state-of-the-art financial solutions for her clients and to contribute to the annuity she is creating for herself.

There are relatively few financial professionals who have Barbara's technical proficiencies; these financial professionals are predominantly insurance agents.

Exceptional Interpersonal Skills

It is no secret that being successful with the upscale markets requires more than technical expertise. Exceptional interpersonal skills are also of paramount importance. The ability to create a strong bond based on trust is a requirement for working with the affluent and with successful businesses. The level of rapport needed to be consistently successful in the upscale markets is most evident among high-end insurance producers.

Unfortunately, there are a lot of jokes about the sleaziness of insurance agents, and the scandals that plague the insurance industry are not helping. On the other hand, no one questions the veracity, the concern, the sensitivity of high-end insurance producers. High-end insurance producers epitomize the concept of being client-driven — which is a significant step above being client-focused.

Richard is one such high-end insurance agent in a most enviable position. For every client he personally takes on, he redirects three or four to others in his agency. Every one of his clients comes from referrals from satisfied clients.

Richard specializes in sophisticated estate management. In a previous professional incarnation, he was a partner with an old-line blue-chip New York law firm. He left the firm, in large part, because he wanted to be able to deliver to his clients a much higher level of personalized service than is possible within a law firm environment. In the law firm he was required to bill for his time — in five minute increments. Richard became convinced that this was not the best way to meet the needs and wants of his high-net-worth clients.

His decision to leave the practice of law and become an insurance agent was a win-win scenario: He is able to do a better job for his clients because he is able to develop the high-quality relationships he believes are crucial, and he is now being properly compensated.

As when he was a practicing attorney, he only works with estates of $25 million or more. The difference between being an attorney and an insurance agent is the way in which he works. Richard meets with each and every family member involved in the family's financial decisions. Moreover, he is often asked to meet with other family members to educate them on what is going on and why. He also works quite closely with all the current advisors to the family.

What is unique about Richard's way of doing business is that he takes the time to truly understand his clients. This is not a peripheral understanding; it is a deep, heartfelt understanding.

Without question, Richard has extraordinary interpersonal skills that make him the "father confessor" for most, if not all, of his clients. He is phenomenally empathetic. It is as if he becomes their best friend. After working with a high-net-worth family, Richard is regularly invited to family functions such as weddings. This is a testimonial to the level of rapport he builds with his clients.

When working with estates of this size (his average being $50 million), all of his decisions are based on people issues. The decisions are not based upon a pure financial calculus. As Richard explains it, "Estate management is about building a bridge between the generations." He sees it as his responsibility to make sure much more than money crosses these bridges.

Some people look at Richard's $25,000 retainer and think it is more than generous. However, given the amount of time Richard spends learning what is important to each family member, the nature of their fears and concerns, and how they view one another, he could make more money flipping hamburgers. Richard's profits come from providing life insurance to deal with estate taxes. The retainer fee is simply to ensure that the high-net-worth family is indeed very serious.

Based on his substantial legal knowledge, Richard employs every conceivable legal strategy to reduce estate taxes. Life insurance comes into the equation only after all the other avenues have been exhausted; Richard considers this the only way to practice. Through these strategies, he is able to significantly reduce a high-net-worth family's estate burden in every case. Only when nothing more can be done does he consider using life insurance. Because of the size and nature of these estates, many of his clients need to purchase life insurance in order to pay the remaining estate taxes.

Richard tends to only work with, at most, three high-net-worth families at a time. He feels that he could not, in good conscience, provide of himself as he feels necessary if he took on more clients.

The Bottom Line

When upscale markets, personal production and doing best by the client are at issue, life insurance professionals dominate. More than any other type of advisor, life insurance professionals have the entrepreneurial spirit, the technical proficiencies and the ability to create a remarkably high degree of rapport.

As the financial services industry evolves, high-end insurance agents will move more quickly up the evolutionary ladder than their peers in other related fields. In the near future, it might be difficult to refer to these outstanding entrepreneurs only as life insurance professionals because of the broad array of financial and professional services they provide. These high-end producers dominate and will continue to dominate the upscale markets.

WHY ELITE PRODUCERS
ARE IMPORTANT TO
INSURANCE COMPANIES

"Don't give the enemy time to regroup; intercept him in his
movements; and rapidly move against the different forces you are
able to isolate; plan your maneuvers so as to be able to fight to
throw your entire army against portions of his.
In this way, with an army half the size of the enemy's,
you will always be stronger than he is in the battlefield."
- Napoleon Bonaparte

"One must not judge everyone in the world by his qualities as a
soldier: otherwise we should have no civilization."
- Erwin Rommel

Many insurance companies have senior management that is more interested in the mid-level producer than in the elite producer. From the management point of view, this preference makes a lot of sense. The mid-level producer is more likely to have established the type of insurance practice that is easiest for carriers to support. The mid-level producer is also more likely to follow established procedures and to make minimal demands.

How do elite producers fit with insurance companies? Consider the following examples:

Carl is the sole producer of his small firm and a member of a producer group. He does about $5 million annually in commissionable premium. He joined a producer group primarily because the insurance companies with whom he was working were not able to effectively support him. In fact, his impression was that he was a bother to them when he needed to move quickly or do something a little bit different from their normal routine.

Fred and Suzanne are brother and sister. They specialize in charitable estate planning. In 1997, they set up 16 charitable remainder trusts with close to $210 million in assets placed in trust. With 11 of the charitable remainder trusts, a wealth replacement trust was also established. Each wealth replacement trust was funded with a minimum of a $4 million policy (face value). Collectively, Fred and Suzanne have PPGA contracts with more than a dozen companies, and each sibling has an arrangement with an independent broker/dealer.

Michael's practice is in the retirement planning field. About sixteen years ago he outgrew his insurance company. His practice centers on small- to mid-sized companies, and he does not talk about 401(k) plans or the like. Instead, he concentrates on more creative retirement plans, such as cross-tested plans and even 412(i) plans. Michael says he has yet to find an insurance company that can keep up, so he uses a third-party administrator in whom he has an equity stake.

Why Elite Producers are Important

These insurance professionals are examples of elite producers, and show that elite producers are important for several reasons:

1. They dominate the upscale markets. Indeed, elite producers are successful because they have created a unique franchise among the affluent and among business owners.
2. They are entrepreneurial — they are the ones who are pushing the envelope.
3. They are able to compete effectively against any other professional advisor, they are finding new ways to achieve competitive advantage, and are an important source of new product innovation.

From a carrier's point of view, elite producers can represent problems. Few elite producers are particularly loyal; they will do whatever they have to do in order to serve the needs of their clients. Elite producers are also demanding, and frequently place demands on insurance companies that often force them to be creative. From a carrier's perspective, it is much more difficult to work with elite producers.

Of course, insurance companies must manage the issue of resource allocation — that is, the extent to which resources should be directed toward supporting the needs of elite producers compared to the broad base of producers. Although many insurance companies talk about supporting elite producers, their actions belie their intent. Qualitatively and quantitatively, most carriers do not support elite producers in the way these producers need support.

All too often, insurance companies do not recognize the value elite producers bring to the insurance company aside from selling the carrier's products. (Conversly, the brokerage units of most insurance companies search out elite producers. They recognize the value of working with these big-hitting insurance professionals.)

So where do elite producers obtain the expertise and support they need to grow their practices? They do not turn to the carriers; they turn to each other. Elite producers congregate with each other in formal as well as informal affiliations.

Expert study groups are one way elite producers share knowledge and enhance their professional development. A more formal structure for many elite producers is producer groups. Producer groups leverage the talents, skills and expertise of elite producers. Many elite producers prefer working with producer groups so that they can work effectively and independently of insurance companies.

A Network of Friends

Some affiliations of elite producers are less well known, although equally effective and influential. These affiliations are not generally talked about — there is not even an accepted terminology to refer to them. The following is an example of one of these affiliations of elite producers.

At the end of World War II, several individuals became insurance agents and maintained their friendship. Their focus was on the small- and mid-sized business market. They became increasingly successful due, in no small part, to their mutual support. As their fortunes improved, they discarded their ties to insurance companies and all moved heavily into brokerage. With their continued success, they recruited new members to their informal network.

What exactly is this informal network? It is not a producer group; it is a collection of sophisticated financial professionals scattered throughout the world. Most of these professionals have incorporated additional services and products into their portfolios.

Although not a producer group, these professionals have extremely preferential deals with insurance companies as well as other financial institutions worldwide. The members of this network sometimes operate in conjunction with each other in order to gain significant business. They also work with each other to support their development as professional advisors.

This network is significant because they have pooled their financial resources in two areas. They have a private foundation that is engaged in a number of philanthropic endeavors, and they have an investment company. The investment company engages in venture capital deals and buys companies for the benefit of the network. Michael, discussed previously, is a member of this network. The third-party administrator he uses and has equity in, is owned by the investment company. All the members of the network use the administrator.

Very few insurance companies are aware of the depth and breadth of this network's activities because they only see a handful of individual successful producers. Because this affiliation does not fit the traditional mold of how producers are organized, they are not well known. In fact, elite producers compose a very small but disproportionately powerful segment of the financial advisor world.

The Multiplier Effect

Many insurance companies tend to be myopic when it comes to elite producers; most mistakenly do not make the appropriate effort to work with them in order to build true long-term relationships. Instead, the basis of the association is all too often simply transactional.

It is telling that few insurance companies see the value in creating relationships with elite producers. Because of their transactional mentality, insurance companies fail to calculate the total value of the relationship with elite producers. Too often, they only identify the direct business being done by the elite producer — how much insurance he or she is selling.

The elite producer is valuable for generating business, for obtaining perspective on the needs of upscale clients and for relentless product innovation. Perhaps most important of all is the elite producer's influence on other producers. This influence is quite extensive.

Most insurance agents want to emulate elite producers and share in their rewards. Aspiring insurance agents want to know how elite producers market their services, and they especially want to know which insurance companies they use for specific products, so they can do the same.

If insurance companies would take the steps to build stronger relationships — loyalty — among elite producers, they would receive a return on their investment many times over because of this leverage. One analysis put the return at an astounding 3,500 percent in the first year. This projection estimates that, for every million dollars worth of commissionable premium written by an elite producer, the insurance agents that he or she directly influences, most commonly through the grapevine, will write about $35 million — *the multiplier effect.*

The Bottom Line

Insurance companies should carefully evaluate and maximize their relationships with elite producers. Elite producers join together to form influential formal and informal networks, and exert a great deal of influence over less successful producers who want to emulate them — *the multiplier effect.* Elite producers are opinion leaders within the insurance industry, and insurance companies should seek ways to develop strong strategic alliances with them.

Without question, if insurance companies want to win the war for the wealthy, they need to work with elite producers. Therefore, insurance companies must understand what these producers need and want and how to best work with and support them (see Chapter 8). Not only will this enable these carriers to dominate the upscale markets, but *the multiplier effect* will significantly contribute to the bottom line of these insurance companies.

8

WHAT ELITE PRODUCERS LOOK
FOR IN AN ORGANIZATION

"Battles are won by slaughter and maneuver. The greater the general,
the more he contributes to maneuver,
the less he demands in slaughter."
- Winston Churchill

"Victory is won by the successful organization of enthusiasm."
- Raymond Carr

Financial institutions targeting the upscale markets for products and services (i.e., life insurance, investments, etc.) find that elite producers are a strategically important distribution system. Elite producers are not restricted to insurance agents. Other great advisors are financial planners, stockbrokers and investment managers. The top tier of accountants and attorneys should also be included. It is just that there are significantly more insurance agents among the best-of-the-best than any other type of financial advisor.

One reason why the best insurance agents are so good, is that generally, they have already significantly expanded their service and product portfolio beyond life insurance. Many have become investment advisors, often fee-based. All in all, high-end insurance producers have become elite financial advisors.

Many financial institutions are eagerly recruiting top life insurance professionals. Not only insurance companies are seeking these high-end producers; stock brokerage firms, banks, producer groups and financial advisory firms are all wooing them. But what do the best insurance agents want from a financial institution, or from an insurance company, or from a producer group?

Extensive research has been done on the preferences and behaviors of elite producers, and has identified six factors that are crucial to the best insurance agents. Financial institutions seeking to recruit and retain elite producers need to be attentive to these factors:

- Compensation.
- Access to qualified prospects.
- Products.
- A learning environment.
- A "home."
- Value-added services.

Compensation

Elite producers want to be fairly compensated for their efforts. The enhanced compensation offered by producer groups, for instance, is a draw to many high-end agents. PPGA contracts and master general agency contracts also fit the bill. These arrangements reflect the inflexibility of the career agency system which enables high-end insurance agents to choose their compensation levels and the type of support they want from GAs.

At the same time, many elite producers are happy with the career agency system and will stick with it. The benefits they receive from being part of an agency significantly outweigh the opportunity for increased compensation.

It is important to recognize that compensation is not the primary reason top producers join producer groups. Direct compensation (the commissions on a single case) is becoming equalized among producer groups. Top producers are looking for more than just compensation. They are very willing to trade direct compensation for value-added services.

Components of Compensation

Reinsurance companies provide enhanced compensation for elite producers. Although this form of compensation should be considered deferred, it is an attractive component of the total compensation package.

Dedicated underwriting is somewhat tangential. Dedicated underwriting support translates into more business closed, which translates into increased compensation. Though seen as a component of compensation, dedicated underwriting is also a value-added service.

Access to Qualified Prospects

Probably one of the most desired factors is *increased* access to qualified leads. Prospecting support is generally more meaningful to many elite producers than direct compensation. Tremendous loyalty is created when the insurance company implements programs that enable their producers to find and work with qualified prospects. Most high-end insurance agents will readily trade-off direct compensation (e.g., higher commissions per case) for the ability to get in front of more people — wealthier people and/or more substantial businesses — who are interested in what they have to offer.

There is substantial evidence that top producers will direct business to carriers that provide meaningful sophisticated marketing support. At present, two-out-of-three high-end career agents will direct business away from their primary carrier on this basis. Even current members of producer groups seek additional marketing support.

Components of Access to Qualified Prospects

This type of marketing support includes:

- Turnkey prospecting seminar programs.
- Brand equity.
- Fee-based investment advisory services.
- Coaching programs.
- Expert study groups.
- Programs for advisors (e.g., CPAs).
- Advanced case design support.
- Sophisticated products.

Comprehensive seminar systems are effective ways to generate new business. High-end insurance producers are interested in many potential seminar areas including retirement planning and distributions, investment management, charitable estate planning and non-qualified plans. It is critical that the seminar programs are truly turnkey; that is, they must lay out all aspects of the process, from how to fill the seats to follow-up and closing business.

Elite producers also value targeted public relations activities that help them stand out from their many competitors. Producers want to create and capitalize on brand equity for their own operations. Insurance companies that increase their investment in agent-centered public relations can make their high-end insurance agents more productive prospectors. A side benefit of such public relations is that it will also result in the recruitment of more high-end insurance agents on their way to the elite ranks.

Fee-based investment advisory programs are also important, as are coaching programs and expert study groups. When working with upscale clients, other advisors, especially accountants and attorneys, are essential allies. Elite producers are interested in ways to create and enhance their relationships with more advisors. Elite producers can employ a number of strategies such as joint-marketing programs, technical support and marketing education. Because these strategies are often so complex, most producers require the support of financial institutions to do most of the work to create them.

Advanced case design support is a necessity. When an insurance company fails to provide case design support for complex situations, elite producers will align themselves with organizations that will.

Sophisticated products are another way to generate qualified leads. These products place the elite producer another notch ahead of the competition. There are two ways of organizing this scenario. One way is to have the elite producer, and only the elite producer, market the product. Thus, these products are proprietary. Another way is to have de facto exclusive products. Because of the inherent complexity of the products, only the elite producers will be able to effectively market them with consistency. Examples of such products include 412(i) plans, cross-tested retirement plans and severance pay plans.

Products

To forestall high-end career insurance agents from brokering their business, insurance companies need to enable elite producers to obtain desired products with attractive conditions. No financial institution builds every product that high-end insurance agents need; some carriers make it possible for their agents to have access to these products through special arrangements. These carriers round out their portfolio by making brokerage arrangements with other insurance companies for products to complete an offering, enabling their producers to have access to those products at producer group pay-outs.

Elite producers also want to be able to make additional financial services available to their clients. Most of these services and products must come through a broker/dealer. The best agents want their primary carrier to provide them with the range of investment services and products they need, such as turnkey investment advisory services, hedge funds and private equity deals.

Components of Products

Insurance companies should make it possible for their members to have access to the insurance products from other carriers under preferential circumstances. Elite producers want their companies to make deals for products and work out an arrangement that is as good as, or better, than any deal that a producer group could provide. In order to provide the range of insurance products, companies should:

1. Conduct a product-based competitive analysis;
2. Identify the insurance products being used by top producers in the career system;
3. Define why they are using these insurance products;
4. Establish criteria for selecting other insurance companies;
5. Create a short list of carriers with whom a deal should be made;
6. Make the arrangement.

Sophisticated products and fee-based investment advisory services are important products. In addition, trust services are crucial to many elite producers. Trust services in particular need to be aligned with the business of the elite producers, and designed so they can be easily integrated into the overall case development process.

A Learning Environment

Elite producers aim to constantly improve their skills, and enjoy interacting with other successful producers. Insurance companies can create value by developing a learning environment, just as producer groups have.

Components of a Learning Environment

The two components of a top-of-the-line learning environment are expert study groups and coaching programs. Both have been shown to make producers more effective and are recognized by producers for the value they provide.

Insurance companies should promote expert study groups because they are a draw for many high-end insurance agents. In a recent survey about study groups, a total of 1,066 career life insurance agents were questioned. Half of the agents did not participate in study groups; the other half did. We decided to look at first-year commissionable premiums as the way to determine the effectiveness of study groups. In fact, there is a significant difference between agents who were in study groups and those who were not.

Study group participants are 2.2 times more productive than the agents who are not in study groups. For every $10,000 of first-year commissionable premiums produced by an agent who was not a participant in a study group, an agent in a study group produced $22,000 in first-year commissionable premiums.

We went a little deeper in the analysis to see if there was a difference in the performance of those in expert study groups versus those in regular study groups. Of the 533 agents in study groups, only 49 (9.2%) were in expert study groups.

If we take out members of expert study groups and compare regular study group members to producers who are nonmembers , we still find that study group participation is related to better performance. Producers in regular study groups are 1.6 times as productive as those who are not participants in a study group. That means, for every $10,000 of first-year commissionable premiums produced by an agent who was not a participant of a study group, an agent who was in a regular study group produced $16,000 in first-year commissionable premiums. Regular study groups have demonstrable value.

But the real pay-off is in expert study groups. Producers in expert study groups proved to be much, much more productive. They were 8.2 times as effective as those agents who were not members of a study group and were more than 4 times as effective as those agents who were in regular study groups. For every $10,000 of first-year commissionable premiums produced by an agent who was not a participant in a study group, an agent who was in an expert study group produced $82,000 in first-year commissionable premiums.

Meaningful differences exist between expert study groups and regular study groups:

Exhibit 8.1 Comparing Study Groups

Characteristic	Expert Study Group	Regular Study Group
Degree of structure	High	Moderate to Low
Use of interactive training methodologies	High to Moderate	Low
Use of outside presenters	Frequent	Occasional
Focus	Products and Markets	Primarily Products

According to the study, no insurance companies now provide expert study groups for their agents. Insurance companies should consider providing this type of support. Expert study groups are fairly easy to implement, and costs are reasonable; agents are prepared to co-pay for out-of-pocket expenses and speaker fees.

Another way to create a learning environment is to develop in-house producer coaching programs. Currently, most coaching programs are offered by third parties. They have been extremely successful in both drawing high-end insurance agents and in helping these agents improve their productivity.

In-house coaching programs have a lot of appeal for high-end insurance agents. Any coaching program should, of course, be geared to the unique needs of elite producers; the process should focus on their business lines.

A "Home"

Almost universally, elite insurance agents want to be associated with other elite producers in a supportive environment. Aside from wanting to associate with talented, like-minded and motivated producers like themselves, they desire affiliation with an organization (e.g., insurance company, producer group, etc.) that they can work with comfortably and effectively.

Traditionally, the only option was the career agency system. Now numerous other options exist, and elite agents are well aware of them. When they make decisions about their affiliation, elite producers say a home-like feeling and top-notch support system is very important. Life insurance companies can take advantage of these feelings by strategically strengthening the career agency system (see Chapter 13).

As one elite producer said in a focus group, "It's lonely out there." High-end insurance agents are extremely interested in fellowship, and this is why top producers are joining, and staying members of, producer groups.

Components of a "Home"

Coaching and expert study groups are effective in fostering the "home" environment. Brand equity in the organization that reflects upon the elite producers also helps to create a "home." To enhance the perception of fellowship, insurance companies should facilitate in every way an environment supportive of the business efforts of elite producers.

Value-Added Services

Just as these elite producers do much more than the minimum for their clients, insurance companies must do the same when it comes to these top producers. Some of what we already discussed (e.g., in-house coaching programs, prospecting systems) are examples of value-added services. However, insurance companies can also add value in other areas.

Components of Value-Added Services

Many of the services already discussed also fit under the category of value-added services. These also include:

- Specialized software applications.
- Agent staff development programs.
- Exit or transition strategies.

Sophisticated proprietary software has always been a defining characteristic of traditional producer groups. In a number of areas, such software creates a competitive advantage. Two of the more critical areas are insurance product comparisons and advanced analysis and presentation programs.

Elite producers are supported by their staff. A value-added service desired by elite producers is to make their staff more efficient. They would welcome staff development programs which would include:

1. Conducting an analysis of the staff's roles and responsibilities;
2. Identifying work flow and integration strategies with the business objectives and plans of the respective elite producers;
3. Providing staff with appropriate training, including their own off-site meeting.

Exhibit 8.2 What Elite Producers Look For

Services	Direct Compensation	Access to Prospects	Products	Learning Environment	"Home"	Value-Added
Commissions & fees	•					
Reinsurance company	•					•
Underwriting	•					•
Investment management	•	•				•
Turnkey seminars	•					•
Coaching	•			•	•	•
Expert study groups	•			•	•	•
Brand equity	•				•	•
Advisor programs	•					•
Case design	•					•
Products	•	•				
Multiple life companies		•				•
Trust services		•				
Fellowship					•	
Proprietary software						•
Staff training						•
Exit strategy						•

The most attractive value-added service a financial institution can offer top producers is an exit strategy that will allow them to realize all their years of business building. Among themselves, elite producers refer to an exit strategy as the "Holy Grail" (see Chapter 19).

The Bottom Line

There is overlap among the various support services top producers are looking for from an organization. Exhibit 8.2 provides an overview of the services sought by elite producers.

Elite agents know their value, and they know their options. In order to sustain their rewarding relationships with top producers, life insurance companies will have to offer more value in the relationship. With all the attention these high-end insurance agents are receiving, insurance companies must take the six factors into account in designing and implementing loyalty programs for top producing agents.

The Changing World
of the Elite Producers

9

THE BROAD-BASED, CLIENT-ORIENTED, MULTI-PLATFORM PERSPECTIVE

"The soldier is the primary and most powerful mechanism of war."
- Jose Vilalba

"Battles are sometimes won by generals;
wars are always won by sergeants and privates."
- F.E. Adcock

The world of the elite producer is changing as fast as the world of the insurance company. More and more, success for elite producers will come about because they are able to position themselves effectively in their markets.

Top producers should ask themselves the following questions: "What am I?" "What lines of business am I in?" "What lines of business *should* I be in?" There are just two answers to these questions. One type of producer adds value by being highly specialized. The other type adds value by being comprehensive. Both are viable positionings, if they are well executed; but the trend is toward the comprehensive approach.

The specialist might say, for example: "I am an insurance agent who specializes in _____." "I am one of the best executive benefits (estate planning, charitable giving, etc.) specialists." "My prospecting success is based upon the fact that prospective clients, advisors (e.g., accountants) and other insurance agents know me for my unique proficiencies."

This is a very viable strategy. There will always be a need for the true specialist. However, this strategy will limit most top producers working in upscale markets. Research shows that more and more elite producers are moving away from this approach.

An insurance agent's ability to position himself or herself as a specialist is difficult because of the increasing commoditization of products and advice. With advances in technology (especially complex analysis and presentation software) and the sophisticated technical support services available from insurance companies and other providers, positioning oneself as an expert is more difficult to substantiate, although it still is very effective for select elite producers.

In order to be successful as a specialist, a top producer must: (1) stay at the cutting edge in his or her specialty, and (2) communicate to key markets, such as other insurance agents and advisors, that he or she is the specialist. Elite producers who specialize must be able to show that the client will receive better advice than what is otherwise available. This is increasingly difficult to do.

The other, and increasingly more effective positioning for an elite producer is to be comprehensive. These producers might say, for example: "I'm a sophisticated financial advisor. I know how to use financial and insurance products to solve financial planning and estate planning problems."

Comprehensive producers bring an array of services and products to meet the widest possible personal and financial business needs of upscale clients. In the comprehensive approach, the elite producer has an area of specialization and co-sources the rest. In other words, the producer would work in his or her chosen area of expertise (e.g., executive compensation) and act as general contractor with respect to other financial services and products.

Evolving technology and technical support services benefit elite producers who opt to add client value by being comprehensive. They are now able to provide an extensive menu of financial services and products. The financial products and services they provide can compete effectively against anything else available.

The Classic European Private Banking Model

Comprehensive elite producers bring the process of delivering financial services full circle. Historically, private banking has been the ultimate in client-centered business. In the classic European private banking model first developed by the Swiss banks, private banking focused on meeting whatever need a high-net-worth client might have.

While many private banks have moved away from this model to a product-oriented way of doing business, elite producers are rapidly returning to it. Elite producers are adopting an intensive broad-based, client-oriented, multi-platform perspective. Their aim is to become *the* forward-thinking financial confidante and advisor to their upscale clients.

Research shows that this approach is working. For instance, the repetitive majority of high-net-worth individuals are seeking financial advisors who are comprehensive in their approach and thinking.

In fact, this approach works so well that top producers are actually selling more life insurance because of it. When elite producers enter the investment advisory business, they write about 20 percent more life insurance than before. Why? The investment advisory business enables them to work with new prospects who would have been turned off to the idea of possibly purchasing life insurance. After developing a relationship, opportunities to provide life insurance usually result.

Clearly, elite producers are reaching new levels of success by adapting the traditional, comprehensive, European private banking approach. Top producers have the interpersonal skills and the means to access the professional talent, financial services and products (i.e., co-sourcing) to be able to compete and win against the best private bankers or other financial advisors targeting the upscale markets. Because many advisors are specialists, a comprehensive strategy puts top producers ahead in the pursuit of the high-net-worth and business clients.

Most elite producers that adopt the sophisticated financial advisor model do so incrementally. However, some are further down the learning curve and have systematized the process.

Integrated Financial Solutions℠

One highly effective and formalized system for providing an array of financial services and products is Integrated Financial Solutions℠, which was developed by Private Wealth Consultants in Toledo, Ohio. Private Wealth Consultants developed a process for working with business owners and the businesses simultaneously across a spectrum of needs. Through Integrated Financial Solutions^{SM}, Private Wealth Consultants addressed seven core needs:

- Compensation analysis and recommendations.
- Key executive benefit programs.
- Asset protection planning.
- Qualified retirement plans.
- Medical benefit programs.
- Employee benefit programs.
- Succession and exit strategies.

Private Wealth Consultants was not able to address all these needs itself, so it established a network of other financial professionals and legal and consulting talent. This network enables Private Wealth Consultants to effectively provide a comprehensive range of financial services and products. In addition, proprietary software was developed to facilitate the process and ensure quality control.

Integrated Financial Solutions^{SM} was not developed from scratch. Instead, it evolved over a number of years as a result of strategic planning activities and client feedback. It was responsive to the needs of existing clients and took advantage of competitive gaps in the upscale market.

Through the use of Integrated Financial Solutions^{SM}, Private Wealth Consultants has developed a stronger and deeper relationship with upscale clients. As a result, client loyalty is stronger and clients resist the overtures of other advisors. The use of Integrated Financial Solutions^{SM} has also resulted in a greater number of qualified referrals. All these factors have increased profitability for Private Wealth Consultants.

For upscale clients, there are many significant benefits of a comprehensive approach such as this. Clients receive financial services better tailored to their needs. Each aspect meshes well with other aspects of the financial program. Financial services are generally of a higher quality. The overall cost of obtaining these services with this process is less expensive than buying them piecemeal.

It is important to note, however, that a comprehensive approach is not appropriate to all upscale clients. Some upscale clients prefer to do their own integration. Such clients prefer specialists. However, more and more high-net-worth clients and businesses want comprehensive solutions.

The Bottom Line

To be successful as broad-based, client-oriented, multi-platform financial advisors, elite producers must offset their weaknesses with strategic alliances, and will need to be supported by insurance companies or other organizations in doing so. They also have to invest in internal operational systems. These issues are just part of the overall strategic and marketing plans elite producers should develop.

In conclusion, elite producers position themselves in one of two ways: as a specialist or as a comprehensive financial advisor. Most elite producers are finding it increasingly difficult to be successful as specialists, and more and more are transitioning into broad-based, client-oriented, multi-platform producers. These elite producers evoke the spirit of the classic European private banker, and are well on the way to doing an even better job than their classic European banking predecessors.

THE COMING CONSOLIDATION

"War is a complicated business that can be mastered only by
intelligence and application."
- George A. Craig

"The end of war is not battle, but the defeat of the adversary."
- Basil Henry Liddle Hart

When elite producers look at the world, the dominant trend they see is insurance industry consolidation. In the flat U.S. market, it has been difficult for insurance companies to grow through internal resources at prescribed rates. As a result, insurance companies are looking externally for growth and are closely evaluating each other (and non-insurance financial institutions) as acquisition candidates.

The consolidation trend is not restricted to insurance companies alone. Elite producers are also going to be involved in consolidation — heavily involved. This consolidation is likely to happen in several waves. During the first wave, elite producers will join each other in order to create critical strategic mass. The second wave will involve the capital markets in the case of a public offering as well as major financial institutions who will become acquirers of these consolidated producer groups.

We are already seeing the effects of the first wave. Producer groups with the capacity to "go public" are already being developed (see Chapter 12). Some major insurance producer firms are looking around for merger possibilities. These events are being supported by very deep pockets, as there are a number of active players looking for business opportunities in this transition. All of this activity is exclusively at the high-end, because consolidators are interested in creating exceptional financial services distribution systems, the kind that would result if you combined elite producers with effective management.

In the second wave, the creation of major insurance producer firms will be very attractive to commercial banks and similar financial institutions. Moreover, the revenues and profits generated by such structures will make them very attractive candidates for initial public offerings.

The Players

More and more financiers and financial institutions are interested in taking advantage of the consolidation wave. Basically, there are six types of consolidators, as shown in Exhibit 10.1.

Exhibit 10.1 The Prospective Players

Players	Contribution	Expected Initial Success
Elite Producers	The elite producers	High
Venture Capitalists	Capital	Moderate
The Mega-Wealthy	Capital, Cross-sell opportunities	Moderate
Commercial Banks	Capital, Cross-sell goldmine	Moderate to High
Investment Banks	Access to capital, Mergers & aquisition expertise	Moderate to Low
Insurance Companies	Capital, Insurance products	Low

Elite Producers

First and foremost, high-end insurance agents and firms are looking to expand their own businesses. Often this can take the form of insurance producer firms merging. For example, Clark/Bardes realized that they needed to broaden their producer base to create true value for their company. Their subsequent merger/acquisition with Bank Compensation Strategies fit the bill. In this deal, it was important that Bank Compensation Strategies was able to recognize full value for their shareholders and side step a thorny exit problem. Because this arrangement has worked so well, Clark/Bardes intends to structure comparable transactions in the future, and has already identified 120 candidate firms. As pioneers of this strategy, they expect to set the stage for the consolidation of elite producers by leveraging their back-office and financial abilities.

For elite producers, there are many advantages to consolidating. Elite producers who are members of these premier firms will be able to provide an array of financial services and products well beyond traditional insurance products. Examples of these products include hedge funds, merchant banking services and selected management consulting services to optimize the value of the client firm. These groups will also solve a major problem for elite producers — the problem of an effective exit strategy. Consolidations create, in effect, a financial services provider aristocracy.

Elite producers are evaluating their consolidation options, and more and more will merge into new and more powerful producer groups and firms. It is important to note that these new producer groups will be different in one important respect from the traditional type of producer group. The new producer groups will not be pass-through operations like current producer groups because they will be designed to go public.

Although not all the elite producer-driven consolidation moves will succeed, some of them will be highly successful. Elite producers are central to the whole process. Elite producers have the experience (through producer groups and selected mergers) to make these arrangements work. They also understand what it will take to make the network or organization a success. The same cannot be said, at this time, for many of the other players.

Venture Capitalists

Capital will be a requirement for consolidation and for creating the necessary infrastructure, depending on the organizational structure chosen as well as the array of support services that will be provided. For venture capitalists, the consolidation of elite producers in the insurance industry looks very much like consolidation in other industries where they have been successful. Venture capitalists are especially interested in buying out elite producers and combining their operations because they are familiar with this type of industry restructuring.

The Mega-Wealthy

Some very wealthy individuals and some family offices are looking to invest in consolidating elite producers. One family office is already purchasing stock in two elite insurance firms, and others are exploring their options. The mega-wealthy are approaching the consolidation of elite insurance producers in the same way the venture capitalists are, and the mega-wealthy should have similar successes.

Commercial Banks

The combination of commercial banks with a network of elite producers can be extremely potent. Commercial banks could contribute capital to build the requisite infrastructure and, most important, create a cross-sell goldmine. The commercial bank obtains an exceptional distribution system for their products as well as the ability to market insurance products to upscale bank clients.

Forward thinking commercial banks are already creating joint - ventures with elite producers and producer groups. Some already have made acquisitions of elite producer firms.

Many commercial banks are conducting cost/benefit analyses on acquiring networks of elite producers, and these banks will be instrumental in the consolidation because of their capital strength and their drive to create a strong position in the upscale markets. Because of the mutual advantages of this combination, the commercial banks have a very good chance of success.

Investment Banks

Save for a few boutique investment banks, most investment banks are not going to be involved in the first wave of consolidations. Instead, they will become more important during the second wave, when the size of the deals becomes significant and when organizations or networks go public.

At present, some bulge bracket investment banks are examining the industry trends and are starting to position themselves to take advantage of the consolidation of elite producers. These investment banks are handicapped in that they have a limited understanding of this corner of the financial services industry. This obstacle will be resolved for them during the next couple of years.

Insurance Companies

The majority of insurance companies will probably watch from the sidelines as the elite producers consolidate. Insurance companies tend to be concerned with a wide variety of issues; a trend in the world of elite producers is only one of those issues. A few insurance companies are taking steps to create programs that work well for elite producers. This accounts for the recent interest in internal producer groups and enhanced services for their best agents.

An alternative approach being pursued by a few insurance companies, and considered by many more, is direct involvement and investment in the new form of producer group. This provides the insurance company with a very powerful distribution system, and is also expected to be directly financially rewarding as an investment.

A Combination of Players

The essential player is the elite producer. All the other players add to the mix, but no other player is critical. Research about high-end insurance producers and insurance firm consolidation indicates that the elite producers will work with one or more of the other players in order to capture significant upscale client market share in the shortest period of time.

Newly forming producer groups are already in discussion with the mega-wealthy and venture capitalists. Some of the more progressive commercial banks and insurance companies are also having preliminary conversations with elite producers. In addition, a number of large insurance producer firms are discussing the idea of selling out to commercial banks while the investment banks are working to understand this corner of the insurance industry.

Obstacles to Overcome

Elite producers recognize an extraordinary and persuasive advantage of consolidation — capital is readily available. When asked about consolidation, many top producers expect that the best insurance producers will consolidate. About five years ago, less than 3 percent of top producers thought elite producers would consolidate. This year, more than 50 percent see consolidation as an eventuality. Soon, most top producers will acknowledge that consolidation is an unstoppable trend. This does not mean that all top producers will be part of the consolidation effort. But all will be indirectly affected.

What, then, is slowing the consolidation process? High-end producers identify five obstacles:

- Top producer egos.
- Lack of access to capital.
- High-end producers have practices, not businesses.
- Viable valuation models.
- Integration methodologies.

While these have some potency now, within a year or two all of these obstacles will diminish in importance. They will function chiefly as a set of hurdles individual top producers must pass in order to join a consolidation project. Let us consider each of the obstacles in turn.

Egos

When large egos clash, very little gets done. When egos get in the way of consolidation, they can block the formation of a cohesive system of top producers that could later be sold.

We all know top producers with burgeoning egos. On the other hand, many elite producers will not let their egos get in the way of their futures. Consolidation activities will seek out high-end insurance agents who have a strategic perspective, who are interested in significantly enhancing their current business, who avail themselves of the most meaningful exit strategy possible and who do not always have to be right.

Incidentally, this ego obstacle was originally said to be the reason physicians would never consolidate. Before the likes of PhyCor, most physicians surveyed said that the egos of physicians would never enable consolidation to occur. Structural conditions favored consolidation despite physician egos - consolidation among physicians is now the norm.

Many elite producers anticipate that the matter of ego will quickly recede into the background. The best producers are astute business people and exceptional entrepreneurs. If consolidation makes business sense, they will look for a model that will work for them.

Capital

Although many top producers cite lack of access to capital as an obstacle to consolidation, this perception is not borne out by the facts. As stated above, there is a great deal of capital interested in supporting a consolidation effort.

Recently, we were approached by a Managing Partner of a London-based family office. This particular family office is currently managing $15 billion for three families. The Managing Partner was interested in exploring the possibility of purchasing a sizable stake in a producer group strictly as an investment. He was looking at an investment cap of $30 million or so. The problem is that presently there does not exist a producer group that can be sold.

From Practices to Businesses

The overwhelming majority of high-end insurance agents have practices, not businesses. Practices do not have any marketable equity. On the other hand, businesses can be sold. Elite producers who fail to make the transition from practice to business will be excluded from all exit strategies including consolidation.

Any steps to move from a practice to a business will translate into greater private wealth for the producer. For that reason many high-end insurance agents are already putting more effort into turning their practices into businesses. No matter how one looks at it, having a business makes good business sense.

Viable Valuation Models

At present, there is a lot of disagreement on how to value a top producer's business. However, a number of major efforts are underway to develop viable valuation models.

International accounting firms, boutique investment banks, leading insurance industry consultants and elite producers all want to better understand the nature and worth of a top producer's business. Most current models overemphasize the numbers and undervalue client relationships and marketing orientation. Better valuation methods will evolve, however, as elite producers and those that work with them get more involved with analysts.

Integration Methodologies

To be successful, any consolidation effort must effectively integrate elite producers in order to create synergy and operational efficiency. The challenge of effective integration will probably prove to be less of an issue in the near future.

Talented people will be available to assist in the consolidation process; their expertise will come from consolidating other industries (such as physicians). Later consolidations will also be able to avoid the mistakes of earlier ones. The combination of the valuation analysts and the consolidation experts will result in breakthrough know-how to radically improve distribution systems for the upscale markets.

The Bottom Line

These obstacles to consolidation of top producers are relatively minor impediments. They may delay, but will not stop, the forces of consolidation. Consolidation is not a question of if — it is a question of when.

Consolidation will come quickly. It will result in a new distribution system to deliver products and services to upscale markets, systems insurance companies must learn to work effectively with.

The Evolving Producer
Group Paradigm

THE WORLD OF
PRODUCER GROUPS

*"The officers of a Panzer division must learn
to think and act independently within the framework of the
general plan and not wait until they receive orders."*
- Field Marshal Erwin Rommel

*"Anyone can plan a campaign, but few are capable of waging war,
because only a true military genius can handle the developments and
circumstances."*
- Napoleon Bonaparte

Since producer groups leverage the talent of many of the very best high-end insurance professionals, it is critical to understand the role of producer groups in the industry. Elite producers have to decide whether they want to affiliate with a producer group or to start one.

Insurance companies have to decide whether to build internal producer groups or to attract more of the business of the independent ones. Clients have to decide whether to work with career agents, independents or those affiliated with a producer group. It is useful to step back and assess the role of producer groups in the industry and look ahead to their evolving role.

Understanding Producer Groups

The three defining characteristics of producer groups are:

1. Composed of a number of independent high-end insurance agents and/or firms;
2. Negotiate special commission rates with insurance companies; and
3. Minimum production requirements.

Beyond these three characteristics, producer groups can, and do, differ in significant ways.

M Financial is the largest, as measured by production, of all the producer groups. In addition to M Financial, there are the PartnersFinancial, the Hemisphere Group, First Financial Resources and Fourth Financial Resources. In fact, more than 25 networks of high-end insurance agents and firms define themselves as producer groups.

M Financial was the first producer group. Because it was the first group, it came into existence in an evolutionary manner. In the beginning, a number of very successful insurance brokerage firms teamed up and established specific types of relationships with selected insurance carriers. Then they expanded their ranks by taking in other very successful brokerage firms and began to invest in systems.

Seeing the success of M Financial, other high-end insurance producers became interested. These agents and firms were not satisfied by what they could obtain as career agents or as PPGAs or even as stand-alone brokers. The new producer groups struck a responsive chord. If they could not reach the minimums required by M Financial or had a different concept, they created new groups.

Although producer groups receive a lot of attention in the industry, it is helpful to maintain some perspective. If all the insurance agents and firms that are members of all the producer groups were added together, the sum would be fairly small —probably not more than a thousand or so. If those agents with only average productivity were subtracted, the number would be a few or so high-end insurance agents and firms. It would seem that in terms of the number of members, producer groups are not very significant.

But, of course, they are. Producer groups are powerful because of the quality of their members — the high-end agents and firms. These are, without doubt, some of the "best of the best" of not only insurance agents and firms, but of any type of financial or legal experts. Producer group members are highly technically adept and are extremely good at building rapport with prospects and clients. Add to this their entrepreneurial spirit, and networks of some of the finest professional advisors anywhere are the result.

The Appeal of Producer Groups

High-end insurance producers are very interested in producer groups. Surveys show that successful insurance agents want to learn more about producer groups. Once they understand what a producer group can provide, quite a number of higher-end producers are seriously interested in joining a producer group.

As a result, producer groups are attracting increasing numbers of high-end insurance agents and firms. As we have seen, this trend is a function of the additional benefits that agents receive as members of an elite operation. This trend is also a function of the dissatisfaction many top producers have with the agency system.

Members of producer groups receive enhanced compensation and other benefits for their efforts. Compared to the career system, members of producer groups obtain a larger share of the first year's premium on sales of life insurance. In addition, most producer groups have their own reinsurance company that, in the long-term, puts more money into the pockets of its members. Another advantage of most producer groups is that they are tied in with a number of insurance companies, and the production from the members of the group is aggregated.

Specialized software tends to be a defining characteristic of some producer groups. Such software enables them to effectively work with multiple carriers. Other specialized software provided by producer groups enables its members to add value for clients in ways other insurance agents cannot.

Still, the number of high-end insurance agents who are currently members of producer groups is small. However, they represent some of the top producers in the world. Interacting with such extremely talented and entrepreneurial business people makes everyone perform that much better. For many high-end insurance agents and firms, a very attractive feature of producer groups is just this sharing of knowledge. Practice support in producer groups is both formal (producer groups tend to have a number of educational meetings) and informal (members get together on their own).

Yet another advantage of being part of a renowned network of high-end insurance agents and firms is the accompanying prestige that generates business. Within certain professional circles, particular producer groups have a marketable image — they have brand equity. This puts their members at a meaningful competitive advantage which, in turn, draws more high-end producers to the group.

As more and more insurance companies pull back on career agency support services, especially sophisticated support services, high-end insurance agents and firms are being forced to seek such support services on their own. For high-end insurance agents and firms, producer groups are quite appealing.

Variations on a Theme: Internal Producer Groups

With all the advantages producer groups have, how can insurance companies compete long term for retaining high-end insurance agents? In the first place, producer groups are certainly not for everyone — not every high-end insurance agent will find the concept inviting. Still, for those high-end insurance agents who do find the producer group model attractive, what should the insurance company do to be competitive? One answer is for the carrier to establish its own internal producer group.

Internal producer groups will strive to mirror the advantages of "external" producer groups. They may provide greater compensation, have their own reinsurance companies, and have the ability to access insurance products that are not manufactured by the carrier. An internal producer group will definitely be an advantage for insurance companies in recruiting top insurance agents. Such a group will be beneficial even when the competition for the agent is another company or an independent broker/dealer.

Although insurance companies can adopt the internal producer group model with ease, they will need to take the steps to ensure that the system delivers on its potential (see Chapter 14). There must be significant and clear advantages to being a member of the internal producer group. For example, besides the purely financial benefits, insurance companies need to develop sophisticated turnkey prospecting programs to be provided exclusively to members of the internal producer group.

Many insurance companies will have problems with this approach because of their desire to be "fair" to the entire agent sales force. It is important to note, however, that when they develop programs that can be used by all agents, the programs have to be built based on the lowest common denominator. All too often the result is turnkey prospecting programs that are too generic, too simple and, therefore, of little interest to the high-end insurance agent.

Although there will be some difficulties in creating internal producer groups, they will become more prevalent over time. A number of companies have or are developing internal producer groups. More companies are sure to follow.

The Future of Producer Groups

Right now, market forces foster the creation of external and internal producer groups. In the scheme of things, they address the specific needs of the high-end insurance agent and firm. But what is the outlook for producer groups? Here are a few predictions about the short-term future of producer groups:

Prediction #1: A Boom in Producer Groups

Many high-end insurance agents looking for supportive professional environments will gravitate to producer groups. As consolidation continues throughout the insurance industry, and as many insurance companies pull back support for the producers working in the upscale markets, many high-end insurance agents will be displaced operationally and psychologically.

A producer group will make an excellent home for these agents. With the growing demand for the producer group model from high-end insurance agents and brokerage firms, there will be an increasing supply of producer groups.

Prediction #2: Internal Producer Groups Proliferate

In order to be competitive with producer groups, insurance companies will be creating their own. They will duplicate many of the benefits of external producer groups. Although there will never be a complete overlap in benefits between external and internal producer groups, internal producer groups will enhance carriers' ability to attract and retain high-end insurance agents.

Innovation should not stop with the creation of the producer group. As competition for high-end insurance agents intensifies, producer groups will move quickly to enhance their appeal. Insurance companies will need to do so as well.

Prediction #3: Insurance Companies Will Court Producer Groups

The career agency system is a very effective way to distribute life insurance and related products. At the same time, it is also expensive. Insurance companies, buffeted by the changing economics of the financial services industry, are looking for more cost-effective ways of distributing their products, especially to the upscale markets. One answer is through producer groups.

Although there are higher commissions to pay, the carrier is not paying for basic training, benefits and overhead. After doing the numbers, some insurance companies will decide that in this way they come out ahead.

Prediction #4: Producer Groups Stretch Themselves to Provide Greater Value-Added Services

In order to attract the "best of the best," producer groups will need to stay ahead of the curve in developing value-added services for their members. There are a number of areas in which producer groups can focus, including more proprietary sophisticated software. This has always been a strength of producer groups. The proprietary software enables carrier comparisons as well as case design and implementation.

Producer groups are also putting more resources behind providing more technical support. Furthermore, some are beginning to provide complex marketing training and related support services, as well as related practice development services. To some extent, the value-added services provided by producer groups are on the road to commoditization. Specialized marketing support, training and related practice development activities will differentiate producer groups as the field becomes more crowded. This type of support will become characteristic of the more successful producer groups.

Prediction #5: Many Producer Groups Will Expand Beyond Insurance

Originally, producer groups were composed of high-end insurance agents and firms that marketed only insurance services and products. Many high-end producers are expanding their offerings beyond insurance into the field of fee-based money management, for instance. There are many reasons for this, but the major one is client demand.

Many producer groups are helping members develop fee-based investment advisory business. Over the next few years, this will be one of the most significant value-added services producer groups will provide.

Prediction #6: Producer Groups Create Brand Equity

Apart from value-added services, producer groups will work on creating a differentiated definable value-added image. This will result in members being more effective in developing new upscale clients.

The image management process will be focused at specific upscale groups and at advisors. Examples of such populations can be based on their line of work, such as physicians, or it can be based on the products and services being promoted, such as succession planning for family businesses. By creating brand equity, producer groups will simultaneously become more effective in attracting an increasing number of especially talented high-end insurance agents.

Prediction #7: Producer Groups Will Continue to Evolve

The existing producer group model is not the ultimate. On the contrary, changes are underway in the world of producer groups that will make them ever more attractive to high-end insurance agents and firms. The move into the fee-based investment advisory business is an example.

Another evolutionary step is the equity model, wherein a producer group buys into a high-end producer firm. The producer group provides extensive back-office support, advanced marketing programs as well as the core benefits of being part of a producer group. What is important is that the producer group is structured to go public. This provides a significant boost in the private wealth of its members as well as a personal exit strategy for them (see Chapter 12). As the financial services industry transforms, producer groups will be in the lead, bringing state-of-the-art thinking and improved ways of doing business to their members.

The Bottom Line

Producer groups are a dynamic and creative invention of talented insurance agents. As more internal and external producer groups are established, competition will intensify for the high-end insurance producers. The producer groups that are at the cutting edge of technology, support services and new lines of business will do better than survive — they will thrive. Producer groups are, and will continue to be, one of the most dynamic and successful organizational structures in the financial services industry.

12

WHEN PRODUCER GROUPS GO PUBLIC

"It takes a long time to bring excellence to maturity."
- Publilius Syrus

"Compared to war, all other forms of human endeavor shrink to insignificance."
- George S. Patton

One of the most salient characteristics of producer groups is that members have an equity stake. Equity is a very attractive benefit, and equity is a principal reason many agents join producer groups.

The attractiveness of equity is two-fold. In the first place, equity means that producers work for themselves and not for insurance companies. High-end insurance agents regularly cite this advantage; shares in the producer group and the reinsurance company are a way for agents to share in the success of their business. However, the way things currently stand, shares in the network are only valuable to members of the network, so their value is constrained. In addition, the reinsurance companies of most producer groups turn out to be, on close inspection, of minimal value. Nevertheless, equity can be built into producer groups.

In the second place, equity is appealing to high-end insurance agents because it provides them with a viable exit strategy. When many high-end insurance agents retire (though the majority end up in semi-retirement for years), their business is over. They cannot transfer their business to others — the rapport with their clients that made them so successful is difficult to transfer to someone else. There is no better exit strategy for producers than having their efforts translate into stock of a publicly traded company. Although many producer groups have stock, it is certainly not the same.

There is also a special case of equity in a publicly traded company, and that is the financial windfall possible by holding equity during the phase of going public. This opportunity dwarfs the current equity arrangement of producer groups.

When a company goes public, the value of the stock multiplies. The multiplier is the Price/Earnings (P/E) ratio. So if the earnings of a producer group is $10 per share, by going public with a P/E ratio of 20 (this is the P/E ratio a number of bulge bracket investment banks have placed on a properly structured producer group), that stock is worth $200 per share. People who own shares in companies before they go public tend to become very wealthy, very fast.

Structuring to Go Public

Right now producer groups are not properly structured to go public. Producer groups are presently structured as pass-through operations. Commissions come in from the insurance companies and are passed along to the producers. An override is retained by the producer group itself to pay salaries and expand the services of the group.

The reinsurance company is the only component of the producer group where revenue is retained. As noted, most reinsurance companies provide very limited equity and are not profitable enough to enable the producer group to go public. Even under the best scenario, they will not be profitable enough to enable access to the public markets.

Restructuring is required for producer groups to successfully go public. This restructuring should result in the creation of a cohesive organization composed of entrepreneurial elite insurance agents and firms. Such an organization would be greater than its individual members and able to thrive beyond them.

This is in direct contrast to the way producer groups are structured today. Now they are loose affiliations of high-end insurance agents. As such, they will never be able to be capitalized.

When properly structured, an organization of elite producers should be a full-service financial services firm. Not only should the array of insurance services and products be provided, such as corporate benefits and estate planning, but additional financial services such as investment advisory services (including private equity deals and hedge funds), and investment and merchant banking programs for corporate clients.

By being part of this organization, elite insurance agents will be elite financial advisors. Many of the top life insurance producers are moving in this direction already. The organization is a means to enhance the pace of this migration and enable the top producers to capitalize their efforts. The keys to being able to go public are: (1) ensuring continuity and (2) the creation of value in the organization.

Continuity

The organization should be more than a collection of top producers. It should be a firm engaged in ensuring its continued existence beyond its current members, a firm motivated to recruit and train the producers of tomorrow. From the beginning, these recruits should be groomed to be leaders in the financial services industry. They should be prepared to compete head-to-head with any other financial advisor from the best investment banks to the best insurance companies.

Creating Value

In order to create value in the organization, the members will have to invest in it by leaving some of their earnings inside. That is, this kind of company cannot be a pass-through operation, but an organization more like the professional consulting firms which have gone public. Elite producers are not opposed to leaving something on the table if they can capitalize their efforts; it is no different than making an investment.

Although elite producers will be investing in the firm, they will also be earning more. Why? The organization will enable them to offer a broader array of financial services so there will be more profit per client. Even without the equity, the revenue projections for members of the organization range from 20 percent increases to as much as 200 percent increases during a three-year time horizon.

A Competitive Advantage

Another benefit of structuring to go public is that high-end insurance agents will be attracted to these organizations in ever greater numbers. As more and more producer groups seek to establish themselves, competition for the best producers will become ever more intense.

Although insurance companies are fighting back by creating internal producer groups and other similar arrangements, in the long run the producer group model will become commoditized. On the other hand, any producer group that structures itself to go public — that creates a gestalt-like organization — will effectively differentiate itself from the rest. No traditional or internal producer group could possibly match this kind of producer group benefit.

The Bottom Line

Going public brings producer groups to the next level. It would probably take a few years to restructure an existing producer group along these lines and to position it to go public. However, after the first producer group is publicly traded, many more will try to emulate the model. Many insurance companies will probably experience an exodus of high-end agents and will feel their power in the industry threatened.

The biggest obstacle to producer groups going public is still a conservative mind-set. If they want to take this revolutionary step, they will have to think outside their usual frameworks. Since they are entrepreneurs, some of those who manage producer groups will restructure. However, it is more likely that elite insurance agents unaffiliated with a producer group will take the next step and create the organization from the ground up. It is only a matter of time before elite insurance agents build the first publicly owned producer group from scratch.

How Insurance Companies Can Dominate the Upscale Markets

STRENGTHEN THE CAREER
AGENCY SYSTEM

"Tactics is the art of using troops in battle;
strategy is the art of using battles to win wars."
- Karl von Clausewitz

"To carry on war, three things are necessary:
money, money and money."
- Gian Jacopo Trivulzio

There is a lot of talk in the industry about the demise of the career agency system. It may be that one day, somewhere in the future, the career agency system may go the way of the rotary telephone and the manual typewriter, but to eulogize the career agency system today is premature.

Certainly the career agency system is an expensive way to market life insurance. Nevertheless, it works and continues to work. More important, it is evolving. What we should expect is not the demise of the career agency system, but a new evolution. And as with all evolutions, some systems evolve successfully and some do not. Stochastic modeling was used to project the number of successful career agency systems into the future. The results suggest that just five to ten strong agency systems will still be in place in a half dozen years. There might be other players, but they will be just hanging on.

Which life insurance companies will be the ones with surviving career agency systems has yet to be decided. The carriers with strong career agency systems in place now might not be the victors a few years from now. It is going to take a commitment to the career agency system at all levels to make it work in the competitive financial services industry. Although transforming the career agency system will be difficult, it is certainly possible. Significant numbers of general agents are making the career agency system a first-rate distribution system; one example is Savage & Associates.

Savage & Associates: A Benchmark for General Agency Success

There is much criticism toward the general agency system these days. Research shows that, to a considerable degree, the general agency system is not supporting agents effectively. This is especially true when it comes to high-end insurance agents. As a result, these high-end agents are exploring alternatives such as brokerage arrangements and producer groups.

Additional evidence of the failing of the general agency system is fewer truly successful agents. The inability of many agencies to recruit and develop talented people reflects on insurance companies and the industry as a whole.

It is very important to understand that the current difficulties are not inherent in the agency system itself. On the contrary, the agency system is an ingenious means of marketing insurance and related financial services. The problem is with the internal operating processes of many general agencies. Research indicates a high degree of variation in the way general agencies are run. With well thought out processes in place, stunning success results. To see this, let us benchmark one such agency, Savage & Associates, located in Toledo, Ohio.

Savage & Associates has won GAMA's Master Agency Award for the past five years. They have done this in the smallest market of any of the award-winning agencies.

Agent Recruiting

Our examination of their process starts with agent recruiting. At Savage & Associates tremendous effort is placed on recruiting the right people. New agents are hired on attitude first and skills second.

The agency is looking for a certain psychological profile, for people motivated by their desire to make a positive impact on the community as well as succeed in business. They recruit people with attributes such as empathy, listening, intelligence and entrepreneurial orientation.

Agent Training

Recruiting is not enough. It is also necessary to train and nurture these recruits so that they become fine financial advisors. Significant resources are directed to training agents, and education and training are taken very seriously. Because they believe a crucial role of the agency is to develop the agent's ability to be a broad-based financial advisor, the training includes technical product knowledge, practice management and marketing.

In addition to basic training, there are enhanced programs and mentoring. Newer agents work with top producers and learn directly from some of the best. Departments such as investments, retirement planning and charitable giving provide training as well as follow-up resources.

Agent Support Services

Savage & Associates also puts significant resources into supporting agents in the field. This is accomplished by promoting them and the agency. One example is skillful public relations programs, and another is highly focused advertising. Yet another is help in creating professional relationships with accountants and attorneys. Extremely well received continuing education programs are put on for these advisors on a variety of topics including estate planning and charitable giving.

Management Commitment

The key to making this all work is the commitment to constant improvement and the attention to process by the management team. Because they believe that the best way for management to understand what agents need is to be an agent, every manager is required to be a current member of MDRT. Savage & Associates places a high importance on MDRT. The first time someone makes MDRT, he or she receives a bonus.

Insurance companies should closely examine agencies such as Savage & Associates. By benchmarking their processes and practices in great detail, they will be able to extend successful models to other agencies. In this way, insurance companies will be able to build agency systems that are magnets for high quality people who will, in time, become top producers.

Clearly, the agency system, per se, is not the problem. On the contrary, the problem is with the processes some agencies use. The lessons that can be learned from Savage & Associates can be applied throughout a career agency operation.

Coaching the Agency

Coaching programs are very popular with insurance agents — especially the more successful agents who want to move up to the next level of performance and production. Insurance agents are not alone; coaching has caught on among all types of professional advisors, from stockbrokers to attorneys.

Why has coaching become so attractive to insurance agents? Simply put, insurance agents want to be more successful. With the traditional agent development systems becoming less effective, especially for more successful agents, they are turning to coaches for assistance.

Coaching is a highly focused ongoing learning environment. Coaching focuses directly on the professional development needs of the insurance agents involved. Coaching is also results driven. Insurance agents who retain coaches do so in order to become more productive. The outcome research of some coaching programs confirms that this happens. Many agents involved in coaching programs believe that they are able to significantly increase their production.

With the success of coaching programs at the level of the insurance agent, the model is now being successfully employed at the agency level. Just like insurance agent coaching programs, insurance agency coaching programs come in all shapes and sizes. For the most part, there are three areas in which agency coaches provide assistance:

- Recruiting.
- Agent development.
- Agency management.

Recruiting

The coach helps the general agent devise strategies to win over prospective agents, predicated on an analysis of the recruiting opportunities based on an assessment of internal processes (e.g., the operations of the agency, the carrier and so forth) coupled with an understanding of the competitive recruiting environment. The recruiting coaching programs tend to focus on helping general agents develop approaches to attracting more experienced agents and other financial and legal professionals who have an interest in becoming successful insurance agents.

Agent Development

Agent development takes a number of forms. Some agency coaches provide insurance agent coaching programs as well. Thus, agent development entails bringing the insurance agent coaching program into the agency.

A variation of this is to coach the general agent in how to coach more successful insurance agents. With the tremendous interest in the money management business, some coaches are helping agencies build their investment advisory practices.

Agency Management

A number of coaches are involved in helping the general agent improve operational efficacy. This can range from time management to the improved use of internal resources to the more efficient use of technology.

As agency coaching is relatively new, there is limited hard evidence of its effectiveness. Agencies we talk to say coaching programs do improve high-end insurance agents recruiting efforts. They do make insurance agents more productive — especially when insurance agent coaching programs are brought into the agency. Also, they are able to help general agents become more operationally efficient.

Where Agency Coaching Programs Are Today

To date, agency coaching programs are conducted with groups of general agents or one-on-one with a single general agent. The group approach is most common with general agents who all work for the same carrier. However, a number of coaching programs bring together general agents from different insurance companies. One-on-one coaching programs are customized to a particular agency.

These early successes of agency coaching programs have not gone unnoticed by insurance companies. One of the most interesting developments is that a few insurance carriers are now becoming involved in sponsoring coaches for their agency distribution systems.

In a survey of 231 general agents, 70.3 percent reported that they would definitely use or seriously consider using the services of an agency coach. That percentage moved up to 85.6 percent when the same question was asked of 142 managing agents. From the perspective of agency managers, such value-added resources are always welcome.

As competition heats up in the insurance industry, general agents are under increasing pressure to be more efficient and effective. Agency coaching programs are emerging as an important way for agents to meet those objectives.

The Bottom Line

Heralding the death of the career agency system is somewhat premature. Still, in the near future, the number of viable career systems will shrink considerably.

Only by committing the requisite resources — especially creativity — to the career system will it be able to survive and thrive. There are many examples of highly successful career agencies; Savage & Associates being one.

Coaching programs are now being adopted by career agencies to enable them to be more efficient and effective. Although the results are all not yet in, the preliminary findings and observations support the value of these programs.

14

INTERNAL PRODUCER GROUPS

*"You must love soldiers in order to understand them,
and understand them in order to lead them."*
- Turenne

*"If we cannot secure our needs for survival on the basis of
law and justice, then we must be ready to secure them with
army in our hands."*
- Mihaly Karolyi

External producer groups, and producer groups evolving into organizations that can go public are not the only two options for high-end producers attracted to the producer group model. Internal producer groups are being rapidly established by insurance companies.

Jason is a career agent with a major mutual life insurance company. Last year, he generated more than $200,000 in first-year life commissions. In addition, he made close to $350,000 in equity sales, about 25 percent of which is fee-based recurring revenue. Things should look good for Jason, but he feels he is at a crossroads. The industry is changing, and he is uncertain how he should adapt.

Right now, he is very unhappy with his carrier. His dissatisfaction has nothing to do with the products. He thinks his insurance company's products are as good as or better than most anyone else's, as is the service around the products. The source of his dissatisfaction seems to be from the lack of quality support that he needs to grow his practice. He has heard there are producer groups that provide the type of support he would like, but he is not sure about making the jump.

Jason is far from alone. He has found that this feeling of dissatisfaction is the number one topic of conversation among top insurance agents. Research confirms that more and more high-end career agents are becoming dissatisfied with the lack of support they receive from their insurance companies.

Lack of support seems built into the system. General agents are usually ill-equipped to effectively support top producers, the home office is not committing the resources to help these producers, and a growing number of insurance companies are dismantling their advanced marketing divisions.

This lack of support creates considerable dissatisfaction that prompts Jason, and top producers like him, to look elsewhere. In increasing numbers, they are looking outside the career agency system.

The Allure of Producer Groups

Robert was the number one producer for his company three out of the last ten years he was affiliated with it. Robert always made President's Club. Two years ago, Robert left his insurance company and joined a producer group.

In the producer group, Robert feels he is obtaining more of what he needs to succeed now, than when he was an agent within a career system. He has access to a number of high-quality carriers and the software to compare them. His compensation has increased for every case he writes. Most important, he is associating with other top producers who are keeping him ahead of the curve.

Robert is far from alone. Many top producers are joining producer groups. For elite producers, producer groups have filled the gap left by many insurance companies. Research shows that producers consider producer groups to be more aligned to the needs and wants of top producers than most insurance companies. Clear about the disadvantages of producer groups, producers nevertheless think they represent a better support solution.

The producer group model is rapidly evolving; more and more new types of producer groups are emerging. All producer groups provide basic product access and client management systems support. Where they differ is in terms of additional functions.

One such important function is marketing support. All producers, including nearly every one of the top producers, are interested in seeing more qualified prospects. Producer groups provide extensive marketing support. For example, First Financial Resources has established strategic alliances with institutions such as Bank of America in order to support its producers. M Financial helps producers market to intermediaries, such as accountants, by holding conferences where intermediaries are educated about what M Financial members can do for their clients.

Insurance Companies Created Producer Groups

The rising appeal of producer groups is a result of insurance company decisions: By not shifting resources to high-end producers, carriers created the opportunity for producer groups to come into existence. Now producer groups vie for the loyalty of some of the best insurance agents around. Unless insurance companies fight back, the "best of the best" producers will either go independent or join producer groups. If this happens universally, it could be a mortal blow for the career agency system.

But let us consider the actual potential for this to become universal. So far, the exodus of top producers from the career agency system is only happening in small numbers. Many top producers will choose to stay in the career agency system because they prefer not to run their own business, or because they believe in the career agency model. Another reason independent producer groups will not become the norm is that senior executives of some insurance companies are implementing internal producer groups.

The Internal Producer Group

An internal producer group provides additional services, products and support to a select group of top career agents.

An internal producer group can initially be costly for an insurance company. It is expensive to put all the pieces in place. Even if an insurance company has most of the components, integration alone could be costly. Insurance companies should adopt a migration strategy and phase in the parts of the program.

Top Producers Write Most of the Business

Research shows that the top two percent of agents in a career system generate anywhere from 21.7 percent to 52.3 percent of production. The range is a function of the size of the career agency system; the more agents in the system, the lower the percentage top agents contribute to overall production. The importance of top producers in the career system is clear. Add to this *the multiplier effect* (see Chapter 7), and insurance companies have a very strong reason to develop programs to keep their best producers loyal.

The Trend to Create Internal Producer Groups

At present, there are more than twenty-five insurance companies that have an internal producer group or are in the process of starting one. Taking a closer look, however, many of these efforts fall far short of meeting the definition of a producer group. One insurance company, for example, defines its internal producer group as the career agents who have a share of a reinsurance company. This is not an internal producer group.

Internal producer groups have to provide services comparable to those provided by external or independent producer groups. If the objective of an internal producer group is to keep and attract top producers, this is the standard they must meet. It is not implausible that a creative insurance company could achieve this standard, but it will probably be difficult and costly.

Although it will be a considerable challenge for insurance companies to establish and maintain internal producer groups that attain this directly comparable standard, no one should count them out. Quite a few senior managers of insurance companies recognize the need for an internal producer group. They also have the skills to create and manage one. Moreover, insurance companies have the deep pockets to establish the infrastructure needed by top producers.

A commitment from the very top is needed to create an internal producer group. Unless this initiative has support from the very top, it gets lost. Furthermore, without a strong commitment from the top, high-end insurance agents will not see the effort as credible.

Benchmarking Against Traditional Producer Groups

An insurance company internal producer group needs to measure up against traditional producer groups. The internal producer group must be comparable to the likes of PartnersFinancial, Hemisphere Group and so forth.

Right now, no single insurance company has all the components in-house; all insurance companies will have to create strategic alliances with other financial institutions. The investment advisory business is a good example of this. Most top producers are very interested in being investment advisors. Producer groups and insurance companies have done a middling job, so far, in helping top producers become investment advisors because these groups and companies generally do not offer state-of-the-art investment advisory services (see Chapter 15).

While many insurance companies are working on the matter, top producers are not going to wait around until the carriers come up with answers. Elite producers are going to create independent strategic alliances with investment management firms. For their part, investment management firms have been responding to this opportunity by providing turnkey programs.

Until insurance companies can build all their own components, they should create strategic alliances and add some extra value to the equation. The extra value will be an incentive for the top producers to continue using the insurance company program.

Getting the Word Out

Once the internal producer group is established, the insurance company needs to get the word out. This involves developing and implementing a marketing plan to communicate the internal producer group to prospective members, advisors such as accountants and attorneys, and potential clients. The key is to create brand equity for the producer group.

Finally, the internal producer group must stay on the cutting edge; it must perpetually monitor its competitors. It must evaluate and respond to changes impacting the financial services industry. It must stay abreast of changes in upscale markets.

The Bottom Line

The benefits to the insurance company of an internal producer group are considerable. A well designed and managed internal producer group can effectively compete and win the business of a significant number of top producers, and will result in considerably more business being written with the carrier. The internal producer group will benefit the production of the entire career system due to *the multiplier effect.*

BUILD A STATE-OF-THE-ART
INVESTMENT ADVISORY SERVICE

*"It is a great mistake to waste men in taking a town when the same
expenditure of soldiers will gain a province."*
- Turenne

"It is not big armies that win battles, it is good ones."
- Maurice de Saxe

Fact: Over the long-term, the fee-based investment
advisory business is more profitable than selling most
forms of life insurance because of its annuity nature
and fee structure.
Fact: Demographic, economic and political factors
(such as the aging Baby-Boom generation) are
creating a burgeoning market for fee-based investment
advisory services.
Fact: Approximately 60 percent of insurance agents
want to be fee-based investment advisors.
Fact: Competing successfully in the upscale market
requires producers to provide a comprehensive array
of financial services, including fee-based investment
advisory services.

Most insurance agents, especially high-end insurance
agents, want to expand into the fee-based investment
advisory business. Most still want life insurance to be the core
of their business, but they want to expand the range of services
and products they provide to any given client. This is because
producers are responding to the needs and wants of their
affluent clients. It is also because it is efficient to concentrate
on fewer higher-end clients.

Research shows that by being able to provide fee-based
investment advisory services, insurance agents will actually sell
more life insurance, not less. Fee-based investment advisory

services actually increase life insurance sales. Although the increase in life insurance sales ranges considerably, the average is about 20 percent more life insurance sales annually. Let us look at two cases.

Richard's practice is primarily smaller family business owners. Richard has found that discussions of business succession and estate planning are often not great ways to get in the door. Nevertheless, because of his persistence and extensive networking, he has built a successful practice.

A few years ago, Richard began offering investment advisory services. He found that business owner prospects, the type who previously were not interested in what he had to say, would talk with him about money management. These conversations led to new relationships. Richard found that the fee-based investment advisory business often opened doors to estate planning and, consequently, insurance sales.

Dale also discovered that investment advisory services lead to more life insurance sales. His primary market is physicians, particularly those nearing retirement. Since it is common for physicians in this category to have overfunded pension plans, Dale would focus on this issue to position his services. Although he was sometimes successful with this approach, he felt he could do better.

Once Dale entered the fee-based investment advisory business, this service was the first one he presented to physicians, and he was considerably more successful in turning prospects into clients. Dale also found that after a few months the physician clients he picked up for fee-based investment advisory business were receptive to using life insurance to deal with estate taxes, with the premiums coming from the overfunded pension plans.

More and more producers are discovering that fee-based investment advisory services are, in and of themselves, very profitable. More important, fee-based advisory services are also an effective foot in the door to the eventual sale of life insurance.

The Attraction of the Investment Advisory Business

The idea of becoming a fee-based investment advisor is especially attractive to the most successful producers whose clients are concentrated among the high-net-worth. There are a number of reasons for this significant trend:

* The significant profitability of the investment advisory business.
* The demand by affluent clients for fee-based investment management services.
* The ability of elite producers to leverage their existing client base.
* The annuity nature of the investment management business.
* The need to be competitive with other types of financial advisors who are encroaching on the insurance agent's traditional businesses.

Profitability

Fee-based investment advisory services are quite profitable with relatively little price pressure among affluent investors. The industry norm is one percent of assets under management. Thus, if a client has $1 million under management, he or she is charged an annual fee of $10,000. The producer receives this fee year in and year out. Over time, the profitability of fee-based investment advisory services outpaces the profitability of individual life insurance sales.

High-Net-Worth Client Demand

The high-net-worth market is currently *underserved* by money management services providers. Increasing numbers of affluent investors are resistant to paying commissions for investment products; affluent investors find the idea of paying a fee based on assets to be much more appealing.

Leverage Current Client Relationships

A very powerful source of clients for fee-based investment advisory services are the elite producer's existing insurance clients. One insurance agent developed a marketing plan to approach his ten best clients by telling them about the new services he now provides. All ten gave him moneys to manage, which totaled nearly $30 million. He now plans to expand his marketing efforts to the best of his remaining clients. He decided that once he finishes discussing investment management services with his current clients, he will look for new business. He estimates that it will take him a few years before he will have to look for new clients.

An Annuity Business

While insurance products are front-loaded, the investment advisory business is indefinite. Investment advisors continue to receive a money management fee for as long as they manage the assets. Keeping assets under management requires great relationship management behaviors, exactly the skills at which high-end insurance producers excel.

Competitive Pressures

Many other types of financial advisors, from stockbrokers to banks to mutual fund companies, are moving in on the traditional field of selling life insurance. It is inevitable that insurance agents who want to remain competitive will want to provide investment advisory services.

The Fee-Based Investment Advisory Business

Forward-thinking insurance agents want to be in the fee-based investment advisory business, not in the business of selling investment products. What is the difference? Although insurance agents have been selling investment products for some time, there is a world of difference between what most of them are doing and being in the fee-based investment advisory business (see Exhibit 15.1).

Exhibit 15.1 Fee-based Investment Advisory Business Compared to Product Sales

Qualities	Fee-Based Investment Advisory Business	Investment Product Sales
Focus	Client	Sales
Service Provided	Portfolio Management	Investment Products
Compensation	Annuity Nature	Transaction

In the fee-based investment advisory business, the focus is on clients and the goal is to do what is best for them. In the process, the insurance agent is compensated based on his or her knowledge and skills. This expertise translates into a service — portfolio management.

The client's needs, wants and attitude toward risk, coupled with the machinations of the markets, are taken into account. The agent is compensated based on the amount of assets under management, usually about one percent. This fee is collected so long as the assets remain under management. As a result, the fee-based investment advisory business is a recurring annuity business. How else can an advisor be compensated for telling a client to stand pat if that is the best advice?

In contrast, when selling investment products, the focus is on selling. When selling products, the insurance agent is dealing with an investment product, which is usually front- or back-end loaded. When the sale is made, the agent gets a commission, then moves on to the next prospective client.

Of course, insurance agents have been selling investment products for some time. In addition to mutual funds, they sell annuities, which are investment products. Even variable insurance often functions as an investment product. For many clients, variable life insurance is a tax-advantaged way of investing in mutual funds. There are many other insurance products that are perceived by clients as investments, for example COLI and 412(i) retirement plans.

Implications for Insurance Companies

Although many independent broker/dealers and service companies are making an enormous effort to develop extensive support and training services, insurance company broker/ dealers are lagging behind. Insurance agents are increasingly demanding technical training in such areas as modern portfolio theory as well as how to prospect for clients and how to effectively position money management services.

Insurance agents, especially high-end insurance agents, are going to move into the fee-based investment advisory business. The issue will be whether the insurance companies effectively work with their agents or force them to seek other support systems.

It's Not Wealth Accumulation

Many insurance companies are moving to provide what they refer to as wealth accumulation services. The problem insurance agents run into is that their upscale clients are not interested in wealth accumulation services; these clients want investment advisory services. This is not splitting hairs; the name of a service positions that service in the minds of clients. As a result, the name chosen for a service is very important.

The problem is that the high-net-worth client and business client markets are not very responsive to the concept of wealth accumulation. Research shows that most affluent clients think that "wealth accumulation" refers to how they generated the assets. A business owner, for example, links the term wealth accumulation to the steps he took to build a prosperous family business. A physician thinks that wealth accumulation refers to the years of study and work it took to become, for example, an established surgeon. Affluent clients think that investment management, on the other hand, refers to what you do with the assets once they have been accumulated.

The Need for Competitive Products

Going beyond the names of the services, insurance companies need to develop an array of competitive products and services producers can provide to prospective upscale clients. Just enabling agents to offer mutual funds is not adequate. There is a vast gulf between selling investment products and providing comprehensive investment advisory services. Insurance companies need to understand these differences and develop programs that will make their producers effective when they go up against other financial advisors.

One insurance company recently rolled out a Wrap account program for its career agents to use, but they are not having a great deal of success with it for several reasons. In the first place, the investment management firms in the Wrap program are all subsidiaries of the insurance company, and do not offer a wide choice to the producer or the client. Second, the fees attached to this program are at the high end of the spectrum, and a great many affluent clients are aware of fee structures. Finally, the insurance company is positioning this program as an innovation, which is not a credible position to knowledgeable high-net-worth investors.

Types of Investment Products

Insurance companies need to provide investment management services that are state-of-the-art if they want to be in the game. The problem for many insurance companies is that they *do not* have the expertise and resources in-house to design and implement the high caliber money management services producers require to be competitive in the investment management business.

Elite producers need to be able to access a variety of investment products (see Exhibit 15.2). One of the keys to success for insurance companies will be delivering these investment products to the right producers.

Exhibit 15.2 Types of Investment Products

Investment Type	Description
Mutual Fund Wrap	Providing a portfolio of mutual funds.
Packaged Mutual Fund Wrap	Providing an integrated portfolio of mutual funds.
Managed Accounts	Providing separate investment managers in a Wrap account program.
Selected Managed Accounts	The ability to bring a client directly to an investment manager.
Hedge Funds	The ability to bring a client directly to a hedge fund manager.
Private Equity Funds	The ability to bring a client to a private equity fund.
Special Situations	Assisting a client with particular investment needs.

Insurance companies have two generic options open to them. They can buy the expertise, or they can joint-venture. Either way, their top producers obtain access to top-of-the-line investment services.

More Than Just Investment Products

Insurance companies need to provide the practice management and marketing support services that are critical if producers are going to be serious players in this field. Ask top producers what they need, and practice management and marketing support are the first items mentioned. Unfortunately, insurance companies have put relatively little effort into developing these support systems for elite producers.

Compensation

Another consideration is the compensation structure. It must be competitive. This is especially true from the perspective of career agents. As an independent investment advisor, an insurance agent will generally receive between 80 percent and 100 percent of the investment advisory fee. If the same individual affiliates with an insurance company, this percentage may drop to as low as 40 percent because of the overhead from the home office and the general agent's cut of the money management fee. With compensation differentials of this magnitude, it is not difficult to predict which option insurance agents will prefer.

The Bottom Line

Today it is fair to say that few insurance companies are taking the right steps to assist producers in becoming successful investment advisors. A large part of the problem is that the vast majority of insurance companies do not really understand the fee-based investment management business from the perspective of those in the trenches. Furthermore, few insurance companies understand what it takes to successfully transition from a life insurance practice to an advisory business where both life insurance and money management are being marketed.

If insurance companies want to maintain their agent-based distribution system as these agents move into the investment advisory business, they will need to redesign the money management services they provide. They will also need to provide substantial value-added services such as marketing training and practice management in order to be competitive with independent broker/dealers.

16

BUILD A SOPHISTICATED CASE DESIGN SUPPORT SYSTEM

"I make war, I make love, I build."
- Henry of Navarre

"Bravery does not itself win battles."
- H. H. Wilson

Until recently, many insurance companies had a staff of trust and estate attorneys who would assist producers in designing complex cases and who were also on tap as resources. These attorneys had specialties; for instance, one concentrated on charitable giving, another focused on asset protection planning and so forth. What made this system work well was that their recommendations were in accordance with compliance and they understood the life insurance business. These resources are being cut back at exactly the time they should be expanded. Consider this case:

Henry is a leading career agent who is debating whether to stay with his life insurance company. Henry's practice is primarily in the field of estate planning, although he is expanding into additional areas. In his estate planning practice, Henry tends to deals with families with $10 million to $20 million in net-worth. He is feeling the competition. Not only are other insurance agents taking some of Henry's market share, but so are competitors such as stockbrokers. To work with these high-net-worth families, Henry needs sophisticated technical support. Although he is quite comfortable with general principles of estate planning, he finds that it is impossible to stay up-to-date in all the many tax and design matters while he is prospecting for new clients. However, Henry's insurance company started to feel the competitive pressure and began looking around for ways to rationalize resources and cut costs.

Unfortunately, their eyes fell on the estate planning attorneys Henry worked with. Because they supported just a few high-end agents and not all agents in the career agency system, they were deemed not cost effective. The analysis went this way. Of about 1,400 career agents only 5 percent of them at most were working on the top end complex estate planning cases as Harry was. Only these 70 or so top producers needed the expertise of these estate planning attorneys. As a result, the estate planning support unit was rationalized (i.e., the attorneys were fired).

From the perspective of the insurance company, the decision to downsize their high-end estate planning unit is a resource allocation choice. With much of its business coming from agents who are not in the upscale markets, the cost of supporting those who are was considered too high. Although it might very well be the right strategic move from the insurance company's perspective, it certainly did not do anything for Henry's practice.

This decision made Henry and the other high-end career agents very upset, for it left them without vital support. For Henry and others like him, the problem is that many insurance companies are cutting back on sophisticated case design and technical support services to their high-end agents.

Henry finds the career agency system to his liking. He has found another insurance company that seems to provide more support, and is weighing his options. He knows agents in the same situation who are looking at other ways to go, such as joining a producer group or setting up brokerage arrangements.

Why Sophisticated Technical Support?

No matter how good an elite producer is, technical questions always arise that help is needed on. Being successful in the upscale markets requires technical sophistication, but even elite producers cannot have the answer to every technical question. They must rely on a technical support system.

Some insurance producer firms have built the expertise themselves by retaining experts and building the case support systems. The costs of doing so are high; only insurance producer firms that have done very well can afford to do so. Other top producers have built strategic alliances with law firms and other financial advisors to access expertise. Such alliances enable them to obtain the input they need without the costs associated with building the entire support system.

The majority of high-end insurance agents, especially career agents, have traditionally turned to their carriers for this kind of support. Their problem, like Henry's, is that it is not as available as it once was.

The Components of a Technical Support System

Just what is a technical support system? A technical support system assists high-end insurance agents in designing the most complex cases. These support systems usually include experts such as attorneys, accountants and other professionals who the producer can tap in order to design the case. Traditionally, these have been formal units within insurance companies.

Whenever high-end insurance agents are asked what support they need from carriers, they always mention sophisticated technical support services. In order to get that support, more and more career agents are brokering business or are switching allegiances to other insurance companies, producer groups and brokerage operations that can deliver.

If an insurance company wants to win business from elite producers, it must be able to provide sophisticated technical support services. In order to attract the business of top producers, leading carriers are building up their ability to provide sophisticated technical support services even as others are exiting.

A number of insurance companies, for example, are recognizing the importance of making available sophisticated technical support and are expanding their commitment to this effort. These carriers realize that there are numerous benefits to their entire career system and not just to the top producers. They also recognize the opportunity to use the availability of such services to recruit experienced agents. The most successful (from a producer point of view) of the technical support systems have five key success factors in common:

- Technically adept.
- An efficient operation.
- An ability to implement.
- High-quality presentation material.
- Ongoing technical support.

Technically Adept

The professionals providing support services must be extremely knowledgeable in their particular fields. In an environment as competitive as the financial services industry focusing on the upscale markets, elite producers must be able to bring the most advanced case design thinking to their clients. Just being state-of-the-art is no longer enough; technical support experts must be innovators, too. The ability to push the envelope will often make the difference in winning a case.

An Efficient Operation

The technical support system must be efficient. Elite producers need quick turn-around. The support system must be able to rapidly produce the case design and provide the supporting materials. It must be as responsive to changes. The faster the elite producer can go back to a prospect with well thought out alternatives, the better.

Technical support services require periodic re-engineering. Developing service blueprints and restructuring to eliminate operational bottlenecks enabling the system to be much more responsive to elite producers.

An Ability to Implement

Of course, the case design must lend itself to implementation. This should be an obvious point, but all too often producers are provided with solutions that look great on paper but are difficult to put in place. The case design must be actionable. Professionals in the support services system need to be cross-trained to work with other professionals to ensure implementation ease. This will mean working closely with administration and money management units.

High-Quality Presentation Materials

To sell a case, a top producer must communicate the plan. Case design and support services need to provide elite producers with presentation assistance. Today this ranges from elaborately bound plans prepared in color on glossy paper to financial analyses which elite producers integrate into a presentation. Regardless of the form of output, the technical support service has to be able to provide accurate information in a way that enhances the ability of the producer to close.

Ongoing Technical Support

In working with affluent clients, producers find their cases rarely close after just one presentation. They will discover new needs, or client constraints, which mean reworking the case design and preparing another presentation. The technical support services system must be able to respond and to support revisions and re-analyses.

Even after a case has been closed and implemented, technical support services must be available to handle ongoing issues and provide backup to the elite producer whenever necessary. The elite producer is focused on building long-term relationships with upscale clients; the technical support operation should be focused on building relationships with the producers they support.

Building a Sophisticated Technical Support Unit

If insurance companies want to have a sophisticated technical support system, they need to allocate the resources. There are a variety of ways to deliver the resources; some insurance companies install several experts in the home office, others have regional centers. In the majority of insurance companies, a single expert or two is the norm. These experts are usually attorneys specializing in an area such as estate planning, corporate benefits or retirement planning.

Proprietary Software

A few of the larger insurance companies have larger groups, and have created proprietary software. Advanced software is a strong selling point for elite producers. They believe, and rightly so, that customized analytics and output provides them with a competitive edge.

Case Managers

A few insurance companies have begun to incorporate case managers into the technical support operation. The case manager is there to expedite (and troubleshoot) the process from beginning to end. The case manager system relieves the elite producer from having to track his or her case through the system.

Managing the Development Process

Insurance companies wanting to develop a sophisticated technical support service should start with a detailed analysis of the current and evolving business lines of elite producers. In this way, the unit will be designed to deliver what elite producers need in the way of case support.

Next, the insurance company must put the pieces in place. This includes everything from operational logistics, human resources, workflow processes design and software development.

Once the technical support unit is operational, it must be constantly improved. To work in the upscale markets, the unit must be kept at the state-of-the-art, and be able to adjust to a quickly changing financial services industry.

The Bottom Line

For insurance companies to be successful in the upscale markets, they must provide the support elite producers need. High-quality sophisticated technical support is critical. While many resource constrained insurance companies have cut back on this type of support, others have started to invest in these support operations. These are the carriers that will draw elite producers and will compete more effectively in the upscale markets.

STRATEGICALLY EXPAND
DISTRIBUTION CHANNELS

*"Strategy is the art of making use of time and space. I am less
concerned about the latter than the former.
Space we can recover, lost time never."*
- Napoleon Bonaparte

"Fixed fortifications are monuments to the stupidity of man."
- George S. Patton

If insurance companies persist in thinking of agents as the only
distribution system for life insurance products, they will miss
significant opportunities. Other financial advisors also cater to
affluent clients and successful business owners who want to
provide a broader range of products and services. For many of
them, providing life insurance to their clients fits in perfectly
with their practice development. Consider these cases:

Susan has her own firm, McAllen & Company. She is a fee-
based investment advisor, and works with two administrative
assistants. Over the last 15 years she has built up a loyal
clientele. About 40 percent of her clients fit the high-net-worth
criteria. Since she manages at least $1 million for each of them,
she is also referred to as a "wealth manager." Susan's clients are
getting older, and they have new needs. They want to make sure
that they and their children are well taken care of. Many of
Susan's clients would also like to leave something to charity.
Because of her solid relationship with her clients, Susan is
being asked to help in these matters. Susan never expected to
become involved in estate planning, but now she is looking at
providing her affluent clients with a wider range of products
than only fee-based money management, and she wants to also
sell life insurance.

Bobby is an accountant in Ohio. He is one of a relative handful of accountants who specialize in personal financial planning. As of this year, he is selling financial products and is compensated by commissions and fees. Before this year, Bobby was compensated at an hourly rate. He did the planning, but the big life sales and the million dollar investment accounts went elsewhere. That has now changed. More and more states are permitting accountants to accept commissions and fees on financial products. Meanwhile, quite a number of accountants, like Bobby, who provide financial advisor services, are looking for the commissions and the fees because they provide leverage.

Additional Distribution Channels

When insurance companies go outside the career agency or classic brokerage system, they often refer to these other distribution channels as "alternative." That is misleading. The career agency system, brokerage, and other distribution channels all work for the insurance company. Instead of alternative distribution channels, we need to think of them as *additional* distribution channels.

Research has identified seven additional distribution channels. They are:

- Stockbrokers.
- Financial planners.
- Accountants.
- Independent investment advisors.
- Property & casualty insurance brokerages.
- Bankers.
- Direct/Internet.

Each of these additional distribution systems presents varying opportunities as well as challenges in implementation. Strategically, insurance companies cannot afford to ignore these additional distribution systems. Insurance companies are finding it more and more difficult to hit corporate growth targets through their existing insurance agent and brokerage distribution systems. More and more are realizing that the time has come to strategically expand distribution systems.

Stockbrokers

In the United States, there are 300,000 to 400,000 full-time stockbrokers depending on how you count. However, only about 10 percent to 20 percent are consistently active in the high-net-worth market. Insurance companies need to focus on these stockbrokers who are successful in the upscale markets.

Stockbrokers are already quite adept at marketing mutual funds and annuities, but they are not nearly as good at marketing life insurance. Although many want to be in the life insurance business today, extensive technical training and support is required to make them effective.

As an additional distribution system to the affluent, the long-term potential of stockbrokers is excellent. With the increasing emphasis of stockbrokerage firms on financial planning, consultative selling and the creation of primary financial advisors, stockbrokers will be more and more involved in estate planning situations and corporate benefit opportunities.

Financial Planners

Financial planners, in general, are already very successful at marketing life insurance to the affluent. In fact, many financial planners were once insurance agents. However, calling them financial planners, as opposed to insurance agents, really is not just semantics. Financial planners have adopted a new professional perspective.

The middle- to high-end of the financial planning world would make a great additional distribution channel for many insurance companies. The long-term potential of this additional distribution system is considerable.

Accountants

Accountants are the number one financial advisor to business owners, and well managed, privately-held businesses are the number one way to becoming personally wealthy. This positions accountants quite well to sell financial services to the upscale markets.

For many accountants there are legal hurdles that must be overcome. Specifically, the ability to take fees and commissions on the sale of financial products. However, this barrier is slowly going away. Still, many accountants — legal restrictions notwithstanding — consider accepting fees and commissions for the sale of financial products to be in opposition to their position as an impartial financial advisor. The challenge for insurance companies will be to identify and direct their efforts to that subset of accountants who choose to sell financial products.

Accountants will need to be brought up to speed on the nuances of financial products. Accountants will also have to be much more proactive if they want to be effective at selling financial products. Insurance companies should expect to provide extensive support and training for accountants.

Accountants are under considerable pressure in their core business lines. This has led them to expand into other business lines such as consulting and financial planning. Insurance companies that work with accountants to help them move successfully into financial planning will be rewarded by a loyal distribution channel.

Independent Investment Advisors

Independent investment advisors focus on managing money for wealthy individuals and families. In connection with personal money management, a significant number of independent investment advisors will take on business retirement plans, foundations and endowments. Presently, investment advisors control about $7 trillion.

Many are fee-based, and some, like Susan, can be referred to as wealth managers because of the way they run their investment advisory business. Although skilled in money management issues, independent investment advisors are usually novices when it comes to insurance. With demands being placed on them by their affluent clients, an increasing number of independent investment advisors are considering marketing life insurance. However, for independent investment advisors to move in this direction, they will require considerable support and training.

Independent investment advisors are expected to rapidly market life insurance when there is fee-based compensation instead of commission-based compensation. More advisors will start selling life insurance that has a level-load instead of a front-load. If a significant number of independent investment advisors eventually market life insurance, the insurance companies that have cultivated this distribution channel will do extremely well.

Property & Casualty Insurance Brokerages

Property and casualty insurance brokers should expand their business to include the marketing of life insurance and related products. They have client relationships, and an opportunity to sell life products into those relationships. To date, however, efforts to develop this channel have not been very successful. This lack of success has more to do with the way cross-selling has been implemented than with the viability of the approach. With the proper strategies and support structure, property and casualty insurance brokers are very effective in marketing life insurance and investments. The more sophisticated firms will be the ones that succeed.

In general, property and casualty insurance brokers are good candidates for cross-selling, although cultural issues will need to be addressed. Property and casualty professionals have traditionally been more transaction oriented than customer oriented. To make a successful transition, a great deal of support and training will be required. Still, the long-term growth potential for life insurance companies is great in this additional channel.

Bankers

There are two areas that have considerable potential within banks: The private banking or trust departments, and the commercial lending side.

Quite a few private bankers and trust officers have believed they have a significant opportunity to provide life insurance products to their clients. However, they have generally not been successful. The reasons for this are culturally based, compensation based and structurally based. Private bankers tend to come from a different orientation than life insurance producers, and lack the individual performance incentives. Unless there are structural changes, do not expect private bankers or trust officers to effectively market life insurance.

Another apparent opportunity lies in the commercial lending side. Commercial relationships, especially those with small, privately-held businesses, could potentially open up personal and commercial life insurance opportunities. Here, again, however, those who have tired it have not succeeded. Bank cultures and structures will have to change before they will be prepared to pursue these opportunities.

What is most likely to occur is that banks joint-venture and even purchase the businesses of elite producers (see Appendix A). This will enable them to be very effective at leveraging their upscale clientele.

Direct/Internet

Going direct, which includes the Internet, will be an increasingly very important distribution channel for a growing segment of the upscale markets. However, it will not happen in the near future. Wealth tends to be concentrated in the hands of older people, and older people today are not as technologically literate as younger people. As the people who grew up on computers amass wealth, they will be more open to obtaining financial services on the Internet, but this will be years from now. Forward-thinking insurance companies need to take a proactive position and prepare themselves for that time when technology and the purchasing behavior of upscale market segments threaten to take producers out of an intermediary position.

The Bottom Line

Exhibit 17.1 summarizes the additional distribution channels.

There are certain additional distribution channels insurance companies should focus on now. The strategic top three are stockbrokers, financial planners and accountants. Each additional distribution channel will require its own distinct marketing effort. In the medium term, carriers should add additional channels, and begin to distribute through independent investment advisors and property and casualty insurance brokers.

Banks are unlikely to become fruitful environments to source insurance clients. The only positive scenario we see is banks creating joint-ventures or acquisitions of elite producers.

Exhibit 17.1 Additional Distribution Channels

Channel	Selectivity	Time Horizon	Requisite Level of Support & Training	Long-Term Potential
Stockbrokers	High-end	Now	High	Very High
Financial planners	Middle- to High-end	Now	Moderate	Very High
Accountants	Self-selected	Now	Very High	Very High
Independent investment advisors	Middle- to High-end	Short-term	High	High
Property & casualty insurance brokers	More Sophisticated Firms	Short-term	High	High
Private bankers/ trust officers; commercial lenders	Clientele Based	Long-term	Very High	High
Direct (Internet)	N/A	Long-term	Embedded Advice	Moderate

Marketing complex, high-end insurance products directly or over the Internet is an eventuality. The key will be the ingenuity of the insurance companies in embedding advice.

Regardless of the additional channel to be developed, significant training and support will be required. This should not be seen as a barrier. Even elite producers require extensive training and support. Forward-thinking insurance companies will use more and more additional distribution channels. The only questions are "Which ones?" and "What is the time frame?"

18

DEVELOP VALUE-ADDED
WHOLESALING PROGRAMS

*"The only way to win a war is to destroy the enemy's forces, which
presupposes an efficient army of one's own."*
- Antony Kemp

*"In war, the only sure defense is offense and the efficiency of offense
depends on the warlike souls of those conducting it."*
- George S. Patton

Consider two insurance companies whose life insurance
products or investment products (e.g., variable universal
life, annuities, mutual funds, etc.) are comparable. Both
companies have roughly equivalent products, both companies
are well rated and the compensation they provide is fairly close.
Each company wants to strengthen its brokerage business
(including PPGA contracts). With the growth of brokers as well
as PPGAs, it is critical for an insurance company to stand out
from the many carriers seeking to market products through this
distribution system. With all this competition, how does
Company A differentiate itself from Company B, or visa versa?

The answer is through the quality of the wholesalers, broker
support staff and, most importantly, the value-added they deliver.
Especially for high-end producers, the wholesaler is a critical
component of the marketing mix. The wholesaler is the personal
connection between the top producer and the insurance company.
With all the competition for the business of successful insurance
agents, wholesalers have to bring value to the producer.

What most wholesalers do for insurance agents cannot be
considered value-added. Value-added is not explaining the
products, pointing to ratings, buying lunch or even handing out
new golf balls. Value-added wholesaling is helping producers
become more successful. It is a model in which the wholesaler

is a "personal sales trainer," a "personal coach," a "business development back-office." Whatever the description, the value-added wholesaler is supporting and educating the insurance agent so that more business is done. Wholesalers can help insurance agents succeed.

Research shows that insurance agents selling annuities and mutual funds who are working with a value-added wholesaler will:

1. Continue to sell products provided by the wholesaler even when the investment performance of those products becomes less competitive;
2. Will sell more of the wholesaler's menu of products; and
3. Will follow the wholesaler when he or she switches carriers.

In effect, the insurance agents are looking for the business development support value-added wholesalers provide. And it has been empirically demonstrated that business development support is often more important than even the quality of the insurance and investment products. High-end producers are extremely loyal to value-added wholesalers.

The implications for life insurance companies are important. Value-added wholesaling will enable them to sell more of their products as well as sell their products to more clients. It will get them the business of high-end insurance brokers and those who are striving to reach the top producer ranks.

Value-Added Wholesaling Services

Value-added wholesaling can take a number of forms. The seven value-added wholesaling services are:

1. Providing sales ideas.
2. Providing insights into selected markets (e.g., the affluent).
3. Seminars for prospects and clients that can be conducted by the wholesaler and/or insurance agents.
4. Making sales calls with insurance agents on their clients or prospects.
5. Technical educational programs.

6. Providing practice management support.
7. Coaching insurance agents.

Let us take a closer look at each of these value-added services.

Providing Sales Ideas

The wholesaler passes along new ideas and ways to sell products. Smart wholesalers are not fixated on sales ideas that sell their products. Their goal is to make the producer more effective; this means any and all sales ideas that can help them sell more. This is the predominant way that wholesalers are adding value today.

Providing Insights into Selected Markets

A better understanding of the markets insurance agents target is a significant value-added component. Market insights that translate into actionable strategies are necessary to result in more business. Also, it is very important to tie these insights into ways that products can be sold. For example, if the insights were about the physician market, then the wholesaler would address such issues as how asset protection planning is a terrific lead into estate planning and the subsequent sale of life insurance.

Seminars for Prospects and Clients That Can Be Conducted by the Wholesaler and/or Insurance Agents

Well executed turnkey seminars are one of the most effective ways of getting new business. By providing high-quality turnkey seminars to producers, the wholesaler is recognized to be adding significant value. Sometimes the wholesaler is called upon to give the seminar; other times they prepare the agent to give the seminar. The seminars must be truly turnkey, leaving minimum discretion to the wholesaler or the producer. This will ensure a positive outcome. Too much discretion on the part of the wholesaler or the producer tends to lead to a muddled presentation.

Making Sales Calls with Insurance Agents on Their Clients or Prospects

In certain situations, agents will ask the wholesaler to accompany them to see clients. This usually happens when the services in question are complex. For instance, one wholesaler is often called upon to make presentations to clients about charitable giving. As an expert in the field, he is able to capably handle all questions the prospect or the advisors (e.g., accountant) might raise. The ability to bring such expertise to the table creates strong rapport between the wholesaler and the producer.

Technical Educational Programs

These are usually in-depth workshops or seminars dealing with the advanced markets. Examples include the latest thinking in estate planning or how to use a family-limited partnership to protect assets. It is very effective when the technical information dovetails with information on how to market the wholesaler's insurance and investment products. More often than not, the wholesaler has brought in a technical expert from the home office or an outside authority to make the presentation. However, by being the catalyst for the seminar or workshop, greater rapport is being established with producers.

Providing Practice Management Support

Most insurance agents would greatly appreciate insights into how to maximize the value of their practice. This often entails creating a more effective and efficient organization. Wholesalers who can show agents how to improve the operations of their practice are recognized as adding significant value.

At the very least, time management strategies are effective and empirical evidence shows that most producers, including top producers, are not managing their time well. More sophisticated practice management strategies, such as the application of equity building models, are in great demand, especially from elite producers.

Coaching Insurance Agents

In some situations, wholesalers act as a coach or mentor to insurance agents. This tends to be very labor intensive and very demanding on the wholesaler. Nevertheless, it creates a very close relationship between the wholesaler and the producer that results in the producer using the products of the wholesaler whenever possible.

Wholesalers who coach agents tend to be more common among new agents. However, there are numerous examples of wholesalers coaching top producers. In these cases, the wholesaler is helping the top producer expand into new areas, such as the investment advisory business or charitable giving or the retirement field. At this level, coaching usually incorporates the other six value-added services. The best wholesaler coaches are providing systematic processes to producers.

Delivering Value-Added Services

As we move down the list of value-added wholesaling services, the demands on the wholesaler increase substantially. The wholesaler that is providing practice management support or coaching services, although quite sophisticated, still needs to be extensively supported by the insurance company. Consequently, few wholesalers are able to work at this level.

It is not a matter of which of these value-added approaches is the right one. They are all effective. Instead, the answer to the question of which value-added services to provide is a combination of the capabilities of the wholesaler and the needs, wants and capabilities of the insurance agents the wholesaler works with.

Some insurance agents will be able to put on a seminar once they have the tools and a game plan; others will not. Some agents will let the wholesaler see their clients; others will not. Some producers will work closely with a wholesaler establishing a coaching relationship; others will not. Nevertheless, nearly all producers are interested in business development support. It is simply a matter of defining what that support is for a particular producer.

The Role of the Insurance Company

Wholesalers are rarely able to build new value-added pieces on their own. This is why most start and stop at the first value-added service — providing sales ideas. To make wholesalers more effective, their knowledge and skills continually need to be upgraded.

Experience has shown that wholesalers can best do what they have been taught to do, whether it is putting on a seminar or making a joint sales call. They are also good for passing around new sales ideas. However, they need the support of financial institutions to develop the value-added programs they can bring into the field. By actively supporting a value-added wholesaler program across the range of value-added services, an insurance company can differentiate and significantly expand its ability to distribute products.

Creating a Value-Added Wholesaler Field Force

Value-added wholesaling is the direction toward which the entire financial services industry is going. More and more insurance companies and other financial services firms, such as wirehouses and mutual fund families, are creating value-added wholesaler field forces.

There are four steps to creating a value-added wholesaler field force:

Step #1: Hire talented people.
Step #2: Build value-added modules.
Step #3: Train the wholesalers.
Step #4: Enhance the program.

Step #1: Hire Talented People

The abilities of wholesalers range widely. As in any field, there are some that are exceptionally good and others who should think about changing professions. The goal, of course, is to hire the best people available, subject to the constraints of the wholesaler personnel budget.

The quickest way to get top talent is to raid other companies. By raiding other companies, distribution is also likely to be obtained. To reach talented wholesalers, search professionals are increasingly employed; however, this is the more expensive route. The slower way to create wholesaler talent is to develop one's own. People new to the business can be trained, or the abilities of wholesalers not yet in the top ranks can be enhanced.

In hiring the best talent, the proper incentives must be provided. A well designed wholesaler compensation system is critical. The more the compensation system is derived from the payout on business generated and maintained, the better. Some of the more innovative models now being deployed emphasize deferred compensation.

Step #2: Build Value-Added Modules

This separates some of the better wholesaler field forces from the truly exceptional ones. These value-added modules make the difference for producers. They are the core that enable the agents to be more successful. Wholesalers, even the best, look to their insurance companies for value-added modules they can bring to the producers. The insurance company needs to develop these modules.

The value-added modules fit into the seven types of value-added wholesaling services described above. For instance, a turnkey seminar program is a value-added module. The turnkey seminar program must be just that — turnkey. It must contain all the elements that will make the value transfer from insurance company through wholesaler to producer complete. Each value-added module must be highly structured.

The following are some of the elements of such a turnkey seminar where the intended audience is upscale clients or prospects:

- A marketing plan that will provide a detailed road map to executing the turnkey seminar program, including the strategies to bring in highly qualified prospects;
- A presentation that is available to be delivered by computer, slides or overheads;
- Prototype scripts for the presentation and follow-up;
- Video and/or audio demonstration of the presentation;
- Press release material customized to each producer;
- Sample participant invitations;
- Handout materials that highlight the producer;
- Follow-up materials, including letters;
- Proposal templates.

It is important that each value-added module be self-contained and fit into the overall market development plan. The best way for an insurance company to decide which value-added modules to build, is by conducting a strategic analysis that looks at competing wholesaler operations, evaluates the nature of the target producers' lines of business and takes into account the products being provided by the wholesaler. This process results in the effective use of carrier resources.

Step #3: Train the Wholesalers

There are basically three areas of wholesaler training:

- Ensuring they have a strong knowledge of the products they promote;
- Educating them to manage the expectations of producers; and
- Running a state-of-the-art wholesaling business.

Every wholesaler must have a detailed understanding of the products and services they are promoting. They must know advantages and disadvantages of alternative products for given situations. They must also know how the products and services work with respect to various planning strategies, such as estate planning, retirement planning and so forth.

Consider annuities within the charitable remainder trust. The wholesaler must understand how the charitable remainder trust works, when the annuity is appropriate, and why and how other options compare. It is also very important that they have competitive intelligence so that when they come up against a similar product from a competitor, they will be able to hold their own.

Just as elite producers manage the expectations of their upscale clients, value-added wholesalers manage the expectations of the producers they work with. Thus, the wholesalers must learn how to work with producers. Working with producers does not tend to be much of a problem for some of the more experienced wholesalers, but newer wholesalers should be educated on this topic.

It is especially important to develop the knowledge base of wholesalers working with high-end insurance agents. At present, not many wholesalers are able to effectively work very well with these producers. Wholesalers who can relate to elite producers as their world goes through dramatic changes will be most effective in establishing rapport.

Structurally, the wholesaling business is very similar to the business of being an insurance agent. In both cases, there is a strong demand for practice management. Education and tools to more effectively and efficiently run their wholesaling practices are in great demand. Research on the practices of wholesalers shows that few of them are optimizing their efforts; they are, for the most part, mistaking intense activity for progress.

By helping wholesalers build a viable business, the insurance company is creating a more loyal wholesaler sales force. Practice management for wholesalers pays off immediately by as much as 25 percent to 40 percent improvement in productivity over the course of two years.

Step #4: Enhance the Program

Any good wholesaling program can be improved. The best way to determine ways to improve the program is by carefully monitoring the activities, the people and the results. Find out what is working well and why, and apply these insights wherever possible.

Additionally, as new research on the best practices of wholesalers becomes available, insurance companies need to incorporate these findings into their value-added programs. Finally, the value-added wholesaler programs of competitors should be evaluated. The things that work best for them will probably also make other programs better.

The Bottom Line

The future of wholesaling is value-added wholesaling. Insurance companies that take the lead in this arena will effectively differentiate themselves from the plethora of financial institutions striving to market their products through insurance agents and other types of producers, such as stockbrokers, bankers, financial planners and independent investment advisors.

Those insurance companies that have exceptionally performing products and can guarantee the performance of their products years into the future do not need to consider this value-added approach. On the other hand, if the objective is to always have a highly motivated top producer sales force, then value-added wholesaling is essential.

19

DEVELOP TOP PRODUCER EXIT STRATEGIES

*"When a general complains of the morale of his troops,
the time has come to look into his own."*
- George C. Marshall

"To gain all, we must risk all."
- Paul von Lettow-Vorbeck

When an insurance agent retires, dies or becomes disabled, his or her practice usually disintegrates. Orphan policies are divided up among other agents; a fair number of those policies lapse. When these things occur, everyone involved is a loser. Clients lose because they are unlikely to get the attention and services they deserve. The producer loses because he or she is not able to financially benefit in the end from a lifetime of dedication to his or her clients. The life insurance company loses because business and opportunities are lost.

For the longest time, the only option for a top producer was to make a graceful exit by ratcheting down his or her practice or handing it over to a sibling. Today more and more producers are recognizing they have another choice. They can develop and execute an exit strategy that not only ensures that their clients will be well taken care of, but will enable them to capitalize the years they put into building their business. Consider these examples:

Jarod is approaching 65. Jarod writes more than $10 million a year. Although he is slowly expanding the lines of his business, he mainly sells life insurance to business owners to help manage the financial aspects of succession. Jarod, like the upscale clients he serves, is thinking about an exit strategy.

Leslie, in the top ten for the last five years, does a great deal of deferred compensation work. Over the last few years he has been expanding his practice from deferred compensation to executive and employee benefits, as well as the fee-based investment advisory business. At 62, Leslie is making considerably more money than before, but he knows that there will be a penalty when he no longer chooses (or is able) to personally work with his clients. More than ever before, Leslie is looking for an exit strategy.

Jarod and Leslie are not the exception. In their age bracket, they are the rule. Moreover, as time goes on, elite producers like them will be the norm.

There is growing interest in exit strategies that will enable capitalization. Research on more than 1,500 producers found that nearly 60 percent of them were interested in developing an exit strategy. Not surprisingly, older agents were more interested than younger agents. Among producers 50 years old and older, nearly nine out of ten are interested in developing an exit strategy.

Few Producers Have Exit Strategies

While there is considerable and growing interest in exit strategies, few producers have a viable one. Study after study has confirmed that few, if any, producers have any form of exit strategy at all.

Among the producers with exit strategies, only a fraction of them are able to implement what they have committed to paper. A handful, no more than five percent, are looking to sell their practices. The problem is that they cannot effectively define what it is they are selling. And no more than two percent of producers are looking to train their successor (who almost always is a family member).

The Producer's Perspective

Studies among MDRT level producers confirm that they clearly understand why exit strategies are important. Nearly all of them articulate the personal financial returns. To this group, the idea of being able to create more personal wealth was certainly very attractive. However, their interest in exit strategies goes beyond personal wealth.

Close in importance is a keen desire to ensure that their clients are properly and professionally taken care of. Most elite producers and agents are very concerned with the well-being of their clients. Most of these producers and agents have worked extremely hard on behalf of their clients for years, and they want someone else with the same level of concern to be there for these clients after their departure.

About half the producers surveyed express concern about their primary life insurance company. Agents want their carriers to be financially strong in order to fulfill the commitments they made to their clients and to them. About a third believe that viable exit strategies are important in order to keep the life insurance industry strong. Recruiting high-quality people into the life insurance industry was cited as being extremely important.

The Insurance Company's Perspective

Not only elite producers would significantly benefit from the development of exit strategies; life insurance companies would, too. Based on a series of analyses, insurance companies would come out way ahead. They would:

- Maintain the flow of premium payments.
- Continue to manage assets in discretionary accounts.
- Provide to insurance agents a value-added service that would attract and retain top producers.

To date, there are only a handful of leading edge insurance companies actively working to develop programs to deal with this issue. The carrier that creates an exit strategy answer will be well on the way to achieving these benefits.

Exit Strategies

There is tremendous and growing interest in exit strategies. Viable exit strategies would greatly benefit producers as well as insurance companies. These are the exit strategy alternatives available:

1. No exit strategy.
2. Sell the practice.
3. Train successors.
4. Create a "firm."
5. Capitalize an entity.

No Exit Strategy

Without an exit strategy, nothing has to be done. The producer or insurance company is already there. Unfortunately, this option does not solve the problem producers are having.

Sell the Practice

A valuation of the practice is the first thing that needs to be done. Different valuation models are currently being developed. Preliminary research shows that most elite producers are not happy with the valuations that experts are placing on their practice. The elite producers believe their practices are worth considerably more than the valuation experts conclude.

The problem with the businesses of most elite producers is that they have a practice and not a business. Practices are highly dependent on the single elite producer; a business is sustainable beyond the single producer. Practices are valued less than businesses, and much less than elite producers would like. An additional complication is finding an interested buyer. Practice goodwill is rarely, if ever, transferable. For all these reasons, selling the practice is not usually possible.

Train Successors

Instead of trying to find a buyer, some elite producers are looking to grow their own. The most common way is for a child to enter the business and take over the practice. Successor programs are becoming more prevalent. In successor programs, an experienced agent mentors a less experienced agent who will eventually take over the practice.

The successor model is being considered by a number of insurance companies. Although it looks good on paper, the successor models have numerous, and usually deal-killing, flaws. This conclusion is based on studies of pairs of career agents who had established this kind of arrangement and subsequently dissolved it.

Although both parties were involved in the decision to dissolve the successor arrangement, it was the less experienced agents who more often were the ones to call it quits. They cited a number of reasons for this decision. The primary reason they decided that the successor model was not for them was because it was not financially worthwhile. The financial benefit they would receive was not worth the effort it would take to properly service the block of business they would acquire.

Complicating the situation is the fact that good-will is hard to transfer; yet good-will is what the junior agents were buying. The primary business of these pairs of career agents is selling life insurance to individuals. Thus, their compensation is derived primarily from commissions on front-loaded products. Although in some cases the renewals can be significant, most are usually not.

If the compensation structure for life insurance changes (e.g. to levelized commissions), then successor agent arrangements will become much more attractive. As the compensation structure currently stands, though, successor arrangements are not very appealing. This does not mean that the successor agent model would not work in corporate benefit situations where there is on-going fee-based business. However, if the business transfer is based on goodwill alone, it is not enough.

Create a Business

If the objective is to sell to someone else, a firm is required. The move from a practice to a business must be made. In a business, a client relationship is not tied to a single producer and no one producer is such a dominant rainmaker that, without him, the practice dissolves.

It takes a number of steps to move from a practice to a business. The elite producer must develop organizational and managerial systems. Additional producers must be brought into the business. These successors must be positioned to take over the business or, at least, stay with the business if the elite producer is bought out.

By transitioning from a practice to a business, an elite producer has created new options to sell. But if this option is not taken, income increases are possible. Studies of elite financial advisors who transformed their practices to businesses have increased their income by more than 150 percent.

Capitalize the Entity

By creating a business, the equity in the business is marketable; there are a number of potential buyers for successful insurance producer businesses. In the near future, commercial banks are likely to be very active buyers. There will also be other elite insurance producer businesses interested in acquisition. Stockbrokerage firms will most likely be acquirers, as will unaligned consolidators. Furthermore, a network such as a producer group can, if properly structured, be capitalized.

The difference between selling the practice and capitalizing it is in the premium the elite producer receives for his or her firm's stock. When the business is sold, the elite producer receives the value of the business. When the business is capitalized, the elite producer receives a premium, a multiple of the value, for the business.

Research shows that elite producers have a strong desire to capitalize their practices. Already, a number of elite producers are working on creating producer groups that can be capitalized and sold for a premium.

The Strategic Breakthrough

The attention directed at this issue is growing exponentially. Although some forward-thinking insurance companies are tackling the matter, insurance agents — elite producers in particular — are the ones doing most of the experimenting. To date, no insurance company or affiliations of producers have developed a workable model. However, the answer is not a secret.

The answer is in *corporatization.* Whether it is a producer firm, a brokerage general agency, or even an entire career agency system, corporatization provides the Holy Grail — a viable exit strategy for producers at moderate and high levels of production.

In many ways, the ability to make corporatization work is the strategic high ground for an insurance company. If products and services are comparable, elite producers will gravitate to carriers that provide an exit strategy. Based on their responses to surveys, there is a strong possibility that many high-end insurance agents would readily switch affiliations to obtain such an exit strategy. Extensive surveys with high-end insurance agents show that just five percent say they would definitely not consider switching.

The Bottom Line

The life insurance company that develops a viable exit strategy, especially if capitalization is possible, will be able to retain its top producers. It will also be able to attract top producers from other organizations. Not only that, but a viable exit strategy will also be instrumental in recruiting new people into the industry.

Corporatization is the answer. Corporatization will enable producers — especially top producers — to derive financial rewards for their success to date. The issue is how to make it work in select producer situations.

Victory

20

SEVEN STRATEGIES
IN PERSPECTIVE

*"Find out where your enemy is; get to him as soon as you can;
hit him as hard as you can, and keep moving on."*
- Ulysses S. Grant

"There is no substitute for victory."
- Douglas MacArthur

There is no question that life insurance companies can dominate the upscale markets. Insurance companies have the financial products and effective distribution systems necessary for success in selling financial services to affluent people and businesses.

The "thing" insurance companies need to focus on is that they need to market their products and services through elite producers who are working with high-net-worth families and businesses. Elite producers are the prerequisite for insurance companies to succeed in the upscale markets. As a result, life insurance companies must implement strategies to attract, retain and enhance the abilities of these elite producers.

Gaining Perspective

In the previous section, seven strategies were identified. These are the seven strategies necessary for life insurance companies wanting to be meaningful players in the upscale markets. How appropriate a strategy is for any given carrier will depend on its structure. It is useful to look at the seven strategies from the perspective of the career agency system and from that of brokerage operations. These differences are summarized in Exhibit 20.1.

Strengthen the Career Agency System

Life insurance companies with a career agency system will need to protect that system. All available data reveals that the career agency system is at its weakest point and there is a need for improvement, especially in the support of elite producers. There are shining examples of the career agency system, but far too few of them.

For brokerage operations, this strategy is moot. By definition, brokerage operations do not need to concern themselves with a career agency system, save learning from the best and subsequently adopting some of their best practices.

Establish Internal Producer Groups

For elite producers who are career agents, an internal producer group that meets their needs is optimal. Life insurance companies which can approach the evolving producer group paradigm will be able to attract and retain elite producers.

For brokerage operations, the issue is understanding the producer group paradigm. A comprehensive understanding of producer groups, including internal producer groups, will make brokerage operations more effective.

Build a State-of-the-Art Investment Advisory Service

Elite producers are expanding beyond the traditional life insurance business. An important part of this move is the investment advisory business. The career agency system must be able to support elite producers as investment advisors. More investment products (i.e., mutual funds or annuities) are not needed as much as cutting-edge investment advisory platforms. Only sophisticated investment advisory services will make elite producers competitive with other financial professionals working in the upscale markets.

If the brokerage operation is already addressing the investment advisory business, it is already positioned to support producers. However, it is likely that enhancements will be required to support elite producers.

Build a Sophisticated Case Design Support System

Being effective with upscale clients requires exceptional technical proficiency on the part of producers. Although elite producers are generally quite good, the field is moving rapidly. As elite producers also extend the range of the financial services they provide, they will need support and training. Therefore, a sophisticated case design support system is needed, and it does not matter if the producer is a career agent or a broker.

Strategically Expanding Distribution Channels

Few career agency systems are able to deliver the volume of business to achieve the desired level of growth many insurance companies are targeting. Given that other types of producers, such as independent investment advisors, are moving to provide insurance products and services, it would be a mistake to ignore the possibilities of enlisting them as additional channels of distribution.

For brokerage operations, these other distribution channels are already part of their business agenda. Brokerage operations need to move into these additional distribution channels to gain leverage.

Develop Value-Added Wholesaler Programs

The future of wholesaling is value-added wholesaling. With the commoditization of insurance products and services, value-added wholesaling provides differentiation and makes producers more successful. Elite producers are increasingly reluctant to accept old style wholesaling. Elite producers need and want business building tools.

The value-added wholesaling approach will also substantially benefit the career agency system. It may even be a major way to strengthen the career agency system.

Although value-added wholesaling programs are becoming a requirement for elite producers, they will also become a requirement for working with those fast-tracking to elite status. Because of the proven effectiveness of value-added wholesaling programs, agents across the spectrum are very interested in these programs.

Develop Top Producer Exit Strategies

The strategic goal; the Holy Grail of the insurance industry. The answer is corporatization. The issue, who will make it work.

For elite producers, the ability to exit and generate personal wealth in the process is extremely attractive. The method would vary for producers in career agency systems and for those in brokerage operations. For example, the producer-group-going-public approach is not an option for a career agency system. On the other hand, the magnitude of the agent's practice will not be as much of an issue in the career agency system. There are key areas of overlap for developing a viable exit strategy; some of these are meaningful valuation models and crucial practice management strategies.

Exhibit 20.1 Comparing the Career Agency System and Brokerage Operations

Strategies for Domination	Career Agency System	Brokerage Operations
Strengthen the career agency system	A necessity	Understand best practices
Establish internal producer groups	An optimal solution	Provides insights into elite producers
Build a state-of-the-art investment advisory service	Necessary to attract and retain many elite producers	Selectively necessary depending on the life insurance company's corporate strategy
Build a sophisticated case design support system	Increasingly a requirement to work in upscale markets	Increasingly a requirement in the upscale markets
Strategically expand distribution channels	Will become increasingly important	Required for leverage
Develop value-added wholesaler programs	Is substancially beneficial	Required for purposes of differentiation
Develop top producer exit strategies	The Holy Grail	The Holy Grail

The Bottom Line

These seven strategies are not the only ones that life insurance companies can implement to be victorious in the upscale markets. A large number of additional, potential strategies have been identified. For many insurance companies, however, these seven strategies are core. These seven should be seriously considered by senior management because they are instrumental to the future of many, if not most, insurance companies.

For life insurance companies to dominate the upscale markets, they will have to distribute their products and services through elite producers. Life insurance companies must position themselves to attract and retain the business of these elite producers.

By implementing the strategies for being successful with upscale clients, life insurance companies will also become more competitive with less affluent clients. The ripple effect happens through the development of the high-quality support services that are needed to work with elite producers. These same support services are very helpful to producers striving to move up. This can be seen in the efforts to strengthen the career agency system; it can also be seen in other strategies. The ability to offer highly competitive investment advisory services will make any agent who wants to compete in this arena more effective.

Evaluations of the few value-added wholesaler programs currently in operation show that they boost production of elite producers, and of all producers. In fact, these programs have been shown to have a more dramatic impact on less successful agents because these agents have a steeper learning curve to surmount and need more guidance.

There are no real secrets in the marketing of financial services to upscale clients. There is marketing science based on an extensive and expanding body of quantitative research. This knowledge is increasingly available to anyone. The critical success factor for life insurance companies is in taking action, in converting the science into successful systems. Frankly, the critical success factor is 1% information, 99% implementation.

21

1% INFORMATION, 99% IMPLEMENTATION
(A Personal Perspective)

"The art of war is the giant among the branches of learning,
for it embraces them all."
- Napoleon Bonaparte

"We are not interested in the possibilities of defeat. They do not exist."
- Queen Victoria

When we work with elite producers and with senior management of financial institutions, Prince & Associates LLC begins by providing the information. This information comes from the hundreds of studies and surveys we have done over the years. With the data in front of us all, we get agreement on what is happening in the market, on who the players are, on the meaningful trends. We assist in working through the implications of the information for elite producers or financial institutions. Then we actively help formulate strategy.

These steps are absolutely necessary. They are also comparatively easy. The most difficult step of all is implementation. Success is 1% information and 99% implementation. The brilliance of a strategy fades away if followed by poor execution. The previous chapter discussed the science of being successful in upscale markets. This chapter, in part, will be about the art.

At Prince & Associates LLC, we initially built a successful management consulting practice based solely on information. Our expertise in selected areas — the financial behavior of upscale markets, the best practices of elite producers, our data bases on the private wealth industry worldwide — proved to be in demand by financial institutions and producers alike.

As we worked with elite producers, we found that they were very interested in the information, but they were even more interested in *quickly* applying the information. Elite producers were concerned with implementation. They looked at our information about the upscale markets and, because of their extensive experience, knew that we were not only on the mark, but had also opened up new opportunities.

Although our information was meaningful in and of itself, for elite producers information is never enough; they wanted help converting the information into activity that generated business. And so Prince & Associates LLC got involved in implementation.

We also found that financial institutions started to want more than just the information. They, too, began seeking help in implementing the insights. They became interested in converting the information into programs that improved the bottom line.

Information is necessary, but insufficient. The move must be made from insight to action. Implementation makes the difference. Implementation grows the bottom line. Implementation will decide the victors in the war for the wealthy.

Moving Parts

Taking information and building successful business development programs is like waging a battle. All sorts of moving parts have to work together. As managers, you now have available different ways we can insure program cohesion; service blueprints, proprietary software, benchmarking and the development of modules. Coupled with leadership, these managerial tools and processes result in deft implementation.

We have all seen excellent strategies on paper, only to see them collapse in contact with the real world. Multiple perspectives are needed, such as those of top producers and the upscale markets. An understanding of the context of the implementation, such as the operations of the elite producer or the financial institution, is essential. Let us take a close-up view of three of the seven strategies and some of the parts that must move in concert.

Sophisticated Case Design Support System

Providing the personnel to manage and construct the cases is the first step. The case design professionals need to be tops in technical proficiency. They also need to be supported by the best design software available, often proprietary software.

A process to manage the logistical issues must be put into place as must the work flow for the internal processing of cases. This is a common fail-point area. Producers often complain about work flow issues using sophisticated case design support systems.

Another moving part is training producers to use the sophisticated case design system. This should include staff training as well as producer training. A critical aspect of that training is when to use and when not to use the system.

State-of-the-Art Investment Advisory Service

A smoothly run back-office is essential. The broker/dealer has to be highly efficient. In addition, the various investment advisory services must function flowingly. The professionals running the platform for the life insurance company must be able to talk to elite producers, have their respect and be quite proficient in the nuts-and-bolts of the various investment advisory services being provided.

Another moving part is the training of the elite producers. The investment advisory business, for example, is very different from the estate planning business. There is a strong need for continuous training of the elite producers, and compliance has to be taken into account.

Value-Added Wholesaling Programs

There are many moving parts in a top-flight value-added wholesaling program; a few will be noted here. Personnel is a good place to begin. High-quality wholesalers are needed; this would eliminate most of the people currently wholesaling today. Remember that value-added wholesaling is about process, not products.

Even after the personnel are in place, they need to be extensively trained around the value-added modules that have been developed. These modules are another moving part. They have to work independently and operate hierarchically.

Training on the modules should be an ongoing process. The life insurance company must continually upgrade the abilities and knowledge base of the value-added wholesalers. An effective and efficient way to do this is through periodic skills enhancement sessions. Internet support services are also useful to keep the value-added wholesalers at the cutting edge.

At the same time, a support desk must be managed. Value-added wholesalers need constant operational backup. The support desk is also responsible for financial product support activities.

Software is employed to tie the whole operation together, and is often developed for this purpose. If nothing else, contact management software is customized to serve the needs of the value-added wholesaling program.

Similarities

For the seven core strategies to add to the bottom line, they must be implemented and implemented properly. As shown, there are many moving parts that have to be synchronized. Unless they are all functioning well, their profit potential will not be realized. One way to think about implementing the strategies is to look at the two broad components — people and process.

People

For any implementation to work, quality people are essential. From the CEO down to the trenches, the people involved make the difference. The greatest strategy will lead to defeat in the hands of people with limited ability. A good strategy can produce great results in the hands of qualified professionals.

Process

The other broad component is process. Top professionals leverage through process; systems are put into place to get things running and keep them running and improving. When things are done properly, the process will continue on track.

Take a well-conceived strategy, add some leadership and true professionals, mix in process and you have the formula for winning the war for the wealthy. Life insurance companies have all the ingredients for victory. The only other necessary ingredient is a desire to win.

Victory

Life insurance companies can dominate the upscale markets. Although victory will not come easily, victory is certainly possible.

The traditional ways of thinking about the life insurance industry, from product development to distribution, are out-of-step with the realities of the global, fast-paced, increasingly deregulated financial services industry. New thinking and new initiatives are required to capture victory. Life insurance companies can win the war for the wealthy — if that is what they want to do.

The Bottom Line: Making the Decision to Win

At Prince & Associates LLC, we have worked with some of the finest corporate leaders anywhere, and they were located in insurance companies. We have seen their unsurpassed innovation and incomparable drive. Many life insurance companies are held back only because they have not yet made the decision to win.

We understand what it takes for a life insurance company to succeed in the upscale markets. The seven strategies discussed will be the critical components. Every life insurance company that wants to have a dominant position in the upscale markets must make the decision to implement these strategies to attract and retain high-end producers and upscale clients.

Of the hundreds of life insurance companies in business today, only a small portion will win the war for the wealthy. The ones that do will have made the decision to win.

Appendix A

Insurance Companies, Not Top Producers, Should Be Worried About Banks

"The capacity of any conqueror is more likely to be an illusion produced by the incapacity of his adversary."
- George Bernard Shaw

"A conqueror is always a lover of peace."
- Karl von Clausewitz

Many people in the insurance industry are alarmed that commercial banks can sell life insurance. Since banks have been effective in selling investment products (mutual funds and even annuities), people in insurance are worried that banks will figure out how to sell life insurance, too.

So far, there is no reason to worry. Banks have not done well at selling life insurance, especially to the upscale markets. Not only that, but they are not likely to be more successful moving forward because of their organizational structure and processes.

Insurance companies, for their part, have been looking over the prospects of a new channel of distribution for insurance products. Banks seem to be an appealing opportunity because they may be a way to access qualified leads for insurance products, and bank personnel should be able to close the business.

Banks have two important expectations from life insurance companies. One is that they will provide life insurance products. This is the easy part. The other expectation is that insurance companies will provide a process that will generate life insurance business within a commercial banking environment.

But there is a fundamental built-in conflict. Insurance companies see commercial banks as allies while insurance agents see them as adversaries. It is ironic because in the near-term and quite possibly the long-term, it is producers who can benefit most by banks selling life insurance. This is especially true for top producers working in the upscale markets, which will be the focus of this discussion.

Creating an Elite Distribution System

The key to success in selling life insurance and related products in the upscale market is the quality of the distribution system. Although there are variations in the quality of the various products, let us acknowledge that they are all still commodities. The ability to manufacture life insurance products is not the critical success factor. Instead, it is the ability to find and work with upscale clients. The need for this ability brings us to the top producers.

Research shows a number of ways commercial banks consider developing elite producer networks. The two most likely strategies are joint-ventures and the outright purchase of a high-end insurance agent network.

Buying an existing elite producer network is the most efficient approach. A commercial bank can either acquire an existing producer group or selected insurance producer firms. On the other hand, a commercial bank could acquire an insurance company with an established position in the upscale markets. Which way will they go?

Acquisitions

Studies show that banks lean toward buying a distribution system without the baggage that goes along with acquiring an entire insurance company. Consider the recent minority stake Chase Manhattan Bank took in USI Holdings. Through this alliance, top producers of USI Holdings will market employee benefits to the bank's middle market clients. In New Jersey, Commerce Bank Corp. has acquired a number of P&C agencies as well as one specializing in employee benefits.

A bank can build an elite network by acquiring individual high-end insurance producers and firms and molding them together. This approach requires an extensive understanding of high-end insurance agents and firms, plus the knowledge and contacts to identify viable candidates. Although this approach makes sense in the long-term, right now it is beyond the expertise of most commercial banks.

Joint-Ventures

Joint-ventures are another possibility. In a joint-venture, the commercial bank and high-end insurance agents agree to work together and divide the revenues from their efforts. The bank and the high-end insurance agents remain independent of each other.

The Benefits of the Combination

In all of these scenarios, the bank provides high-end agents with qualified leads. Agents are also given access to a wider range of financial products on which they are compensated. If commercial banks acquire the high-end insurance agent networks, they provide an exit strategy for these top producers. Based on current financial models, this arrangement will significantly capitalize the practices of top producers.

Clearly, the top producers can do quite well with this arrangement. But what about the banks?

Benefits to the Banks

The banks do quite well too. First and foremost, the commercial bank gets the finest financial services distribution system geared to the upscale markets. Not only will this distribution system enable the bank to effectively market life insurance products to its existing clientele and new clients, but it will be many times more effective in marketing related financial products, such as investment management services. Research shows that high-end insurance agents are better at marketing an array of investment products to high-net-worth individuals than are private bankers and trust officers.

Banks would not be limited to cross-selling investment management. They could very well empower agents to cross-sell everything from credit and transaction services to investment and merchant banking services. For the upscale markets, this distribution system would enable commercial banks to effectively leverage their services, products and relationships.

This arrangement will also provide the commercial bank with many new upscale clients. The roster of current upscale clients of the high-end insurance agents will be prime candidates for the services and products of the bank. Top producers are more effective at prospecting the upscale markets than any other type of financial advisor, including private bankers and trust officers. Top producers can be expected to generate new clients for the bank.

Banks will also profit from the sale of life insurance. Banks have not been effective life insurance marketers as yet, so these will be incremental revenues. By being aligned with a high-end insurance agent network, commercial banks will be able to compete against all comers.

Commercial banks can attain these positive outcomes by skimming off the "best of the best" insurance agents. With their package of new clients, more products and a viable exit strategy, commercial banks will be able to draw from the top two percent of elite producers. In effect, commercial banks could create their own state-of-the-art producer group, which will be quite attractive to elite producers.

Implications for Insurance Companies

In the event that commercial banks develop these elite producer distribution systems, insurance companies will find it far less profitable to work with them. Commercial banks are likely to quickly move into the underwriting business. If the banks have this elite producer network, the odds of success as an underwriter are quite good. A logical next step would be to purchase insurance companies in order to vertically integrate.

Culture Clash

The only significant obstacle to banks being able to create elite producer distribution systems is a likely clash of cultures. High-end insurance agents have a very different culture than bankers. Conflicts might occur when elite producers and bankers have to work together.

Managing a culture clash in this environment is not too difficult. A facilitator is needed to help both sides understand each other. The facilitator should be comfortable in both worlds — banking and insurance. The facilitator works with private bankers, trust officers, commercial lenders and so forth to access the qualified leads from the bank. He or she tracks the process through to the closing of business by the elite producer.

All the while, the facilitator resolves the issues that arise. With the services of a facilitator, the benefits of partnerships between banks and high-end insurance agents exceed any drawbacks.

The Bottom Line

In sum, the concern about banks is misplaced. Many high-end insurance agents will significantly benefit from commercial banks entering the life insurance business, and the commercial banks will benefit as well.

On the other hand, insurance companies will not fare as well. In the short-term, many will be pressured to cut costs and deliver exceptional (and expensive) service levels. In the long-term, they may very well become subsidiaries of bank holding companies.

For some insurance companies, this scenario is very attractive. These carriers will position themselves to take advantage of the eventual consolidation. On the other hand, this scenario is much less attractive for most carriers.

In order to sustain their competitive advantage, insurance companies will have to protect their superior distribution channels to the upscale markets. The window of opportunity for these life insurance companies is slowly closing. If action is not taken in the next few years, banks may very well be the dominant financial institution selling life insurance to the upscale markets.

Appendix B

It's Not a Better Mouse Trap — It's More Enticing Cheese

"There is no room in war for delicate machinery."
- Archibald Wavell

"If you load a mud foot down with a lot of gadgets that he has to watch, somebody a lot more simply equipped - say with a stone ax - will sneak up and bash his head in while he is trying to read a venire."
- Robert Heinlein

Insurance companies have repeatedly proven themselves to be deft technical innovators in creating financial products. Despite their technical abilities, however, many financial products have not met their projections. Examples of this success gap include cross-tested retirement plans, the 412(i) plan, the charitable remainder trust and insurance carriers' trust companies.

At present, insurance companies are on the verge of creating another generation of technically excellent products that may also meet with difficulties in the marketplace. One of these is the next generation of retirement products. These should be in great demand. These products are a significant evolution from what is currently available because they are designed to benefit the investor, the insurance agent and the insurance company.

This generation of products will make adroit use of the tax code, the latest thinking in modern portfolio theory, and an extensive in-depth understanding of the pre-retirement market. These products will also have a number of characteristics that will make them unique. They will have extensive operational versatility and bring the expertise previously restricted to the very wealthy to the average investor. The operational versatility will enable the retirement product to solve broader financial needs.

This new generation of retirement products plus is operationally complex, requiring the services of financial advisors to assist retirement investors in customizing them to meet individual needs and wants. Financial advisors will be instrumental in the design phase, and must subsequently monitor, evaluate and modify investment decisions.

One might think that once these innovative retirement programs are rolled out, sales and profits are assured. Unfortunately, this probably will not happen.

Why? Because many of the insurance companies are concentrating only on the technical aspects of these products; sales, marketing and customer considerations are not being taken into account. This flaw in the new product development process is not limited to insurance companies. It is characteristic of the entire financial services industry. Financial institutions, from banks to wirehouses to insurance companies, build products and expect the marketing department and the sales force to then bring in the customers.

This is a risky expectation. Because of the technical requirements, product development is a combination of actuarial analyses, legal explication, systems support and so forth. It can cost millions of dollars to develop a new financial product. All too often, we see the new product ball passed off with no one there to catch it.

The Need for Multi-Function New Product Teams

With all this in mind, consider the advantages of multifunctional new product teams. Imagine the marketing systems designed as the technical aspects are assembled. An absolutely critical success factor of the financial product is the front-end marketing system.

The Front-End Marketing System

Insurance companies should put more effort into creating the marketing/sales tools and programs with which their producers can access qualified prospects and close business more easily. These tools and programs would be developed to leverage the logic behind building the financial products and would be predicated on the buying psychology of the target client. For instance, among the upscale markets, the use of high-net-worth psychology is essential.

The Bottom Line

In sum, when building new financial products, insurance companies should also think about building the sales and marketing front-end. At the same time, front-ends should be built for existing products. Instead of simply relying on the sales force to sell, properly equipping them will make existing financial products that much more successful.

It's not enough to build a better mouse trap. What's needed is more enticing cheese.

Appendix C
Getting the Most from Strategy Consultants

"Nobody ever went broke supplying an army."
- Fletcher Pratt

"Diplomacy without armaments is like music without instruments."
- Fredrick the Great

Many types of management consultants are employed by insurance companies. Technology consultants, for example, are in high demand because of the need to effectively use technology to improve operations, create competitive advantage and add value. Training consultants are frequently called in because of the need for constant improvement in the skills of employees and the field force. Strategy consultants are sought out because of the high-speed changes that are now characteristic of the financial services industry. The domains of these consultants can overlap; the focus here will be on strategy consultants and how to get the most from them.

Strategy consultants advise senior officers of insurance companies about the financial services industry and how to position their company to compete most effectively. They help senior management chart a direction by bringing their expertise to bear on specific concerns and/or the overall direction of the company, including such issues as mergers, acquisitions and strategic alliances.

For Better or Worse

With the changes impacting the insurance industry, more and more CEOs are calling in strategy consultants to help them chart a course or provide an external assessment of internal direction setting. Calling in a strategy consultant can be a very wise move, provided senior management takes the proper steps in working with their chosen consulting firm. Calling in the wrong strategy consultant, however, or mismanaging the work of any consultant, creates adverse consequences for the carrier. The company may subsequently make a poor decision or overlook meaningful opportunities.

The work of strategy consultants either turns out well or very poorly. When it turns out poorly, the responsibility is that of the CEO and senior management. For a company to protect itself against this type of failure, it is useful to understand why some strategy consultants fail to deliver. Three guidelines will then be presented for getting the most from strategy consultants.

Why Strategy Consultants Fail to Deliver

In every profession there are those who are simply incompetent, and their work shows it. One has to be careful whom one hires (see Guideline #1 below). The real problem is that even some of the most knowledgeable strategy consultants prove to be disastrous for their clients. Let us look at why some very knowledgeable, very capable strategy consultants fail to deliver what they promise — viable solutions to significant problems.

The reason some talented strategy consultants fail to deliver often lies in their fascination with ideas. This fascination with ideas led them to being strategy consultants in the first place. Tough problems have a compelling attraction for strategy consultants. Strategic problems are like many other intellectual puzzles; the fun is in the process of working through to the solution. This fascination with the process leads to the consultant's malady: "analysis paralysis." The ideas become so enthralling that implementation becomes an afterthought.

Many strategy consultants do not stay around for the often messy work of implementation. Instead, they move on to the next fascinating problem. As a result, it is easy to get disconnected from the real world, but the real world is where insurance companies will win or lose.

Our own experience at Prince & Associates LLC bears this out. We are often called upon to assist and facilitate strategy development for insurance companies intent on attracting and delivering support services for high-end producers. Our success in these engagements is a product of extensive empirical work in the area and years of implementation work with elite producers.

A number of the best (as measured by annual production) life insurance producers (firms and individuals) in the industry are our clients. We help them significantly enhance the value of their practices. This often takes the form of delivering practice management services, developing marketing programs that target upscale clients, providing guidance, helping these producers forge strategic alliances and perhaps even merge their firms or acquire other firms.

We also periodically work with life insurance producers to design and present proposals to upscale clients. For example, on behalf of certain elite producers, we make presentations to their high-net-worth clients on how to establish and run private foundations.

By working closely with elite producers, we gain insights that broad-based empirical research alone could never provide. In other words, the perspective from the trenches is very different from that of a map of the battlefield. Only by putting in years of work with elite producers have we been able to intimately understand their world. These insights enable us to bring a more comprehensive and detailed perspective to our strategy consulting engagements with insurance companies. It is the nuances that often make all the difference.

In a similar vein, some strategy consultants underestimate the distance between determining the solution and fixing the problem. It is much easier to tell someone how to make things work better than to actually put it into practice. This is the difference between theory and action, between fancy reports and first-rate results.

At Prince & Associates LLC, we firmly believe that if strategy consultants had to implement everything they wrote, they would easily write ten times less — no, more likely twenty times less. Reports and presentations to senior management are part and parcel of the job of strategy consultants, but moving from paper to performance is the critical element. In this area, a number of strategy consultants fall dreadfully short.

We regularly become involved with insurance companies for extended periods of time. After helping in strategy development, we are usually called upon to help with implementation. This is where all the theory, all the ideas, all the analyses are translated into action. This is how we are judged because, in the end, we have to show that we have been able to improve the insurance company's bottom line by a large multiple of our fees.

This is how all consultants should to be judged. In the final analysis, results are what matter. When we work with elite producers, results are all that matter. When it comes to our work with producers, our results are easy to assess. If we could not help top producers generate significantly more profit above and beyond our fees, then these producers would quickly drop us. Instead, they usually prefer to put us on long-term retainers.

Guidelines for Getting the Most from Your Strategy Consultants

You can avoid disasters. You can avoid a waste of resources. You can obtain results to make your insurance company more successful. In working with strategy consultants, you need to follow three key guidelines:

- Guideline #1: Carefully select the strategy consulting firm.
- Guideline #2: Set the parameters of the strategy consulting engagement.
- Guideline #3: Make the strategy consulting engagement a partnership.

Guideline #1: Carefully Select the Strategy Consulting Firm

Due diligence is a cornerstone of an elite producer's practice. It should also be the cornerstone of selecting a strategy consultant. This guideline is critical if you want to get the most from your strategy consultant.

Some of the ways strategy consultants are selected include: (1) track record, (2) the name of the consulting firm and (3) recognized expertise. In all cases, the objective is to access the best talent to help you design and implement corporate strategy or conduct specific projects. Each of these approaches can result in finding that talent.

A strategy consulting firm's track record in the insurance industry is a good indication of its ability to help you. The only problem with this is that some strategy consulting firms engage, intentionally or unintentionally, in a bait-and-switch approach to marketing. They talk about how the strategy consulting firm has "done this type of work in the past" or "has the expertise to help you set your company's direction."

The real questions are "Who did the work?" and "Which people within the consulting firm did the work, and where are they now?" You want the people with the track record to be the ones working for you.

Remember the old joke: "What's a consultant? A consultant borrows your watch to tell you the time and keeps the watch." If all they did was pick the brains of your best people and report it back to you, then you are certainly wasting time and money—your time and money.

It is not uncommon for an insurance company to pick a consultant based on the name of the firm. If you select a name firm, board members and others will be less likely to criticize your choice. But the name firm may not be able to provide the skilled people you require to do the job. The breadth and depth of a firm's personnel is more important than its name. It is not the firm that will do the work, it is the people.

Another choice you must often make is whether to choose a large multi-faceted strategy consulting firm or a boutique firm. As boutique strategy consultants, Prince & Associates LLC is limited to working with insurance companies in selected areas. These are the areas where we have the requisite expertise and implementation skills to add meaningfully to the bottom line of our insurance company clients.

Our areas of expertise center on the upscale markets. We know the products and services and the marketing programs that compliment them. We also know the distribution systems used to reach the upscale markets. Because of this expertise, we concentrate on organizational issues, business management practices and marketing matters, as well as selected mergers and acquisition situations. We also assist in the establishment of strategic alliances that help top producers and insurance companies find and service upscale clients. And, perhaps most important, we stay away from what we do not know.

Recently, we were approached by an insurance company to work on pricing issues for their mutual fund complex; we referred them to another consulting firm. Another time, we were asked to help in establishing a reinsurance company. Once again, we needed to refer this business to others. When a strategy consulting firm moves outside its domain of expertise, it is likely to be ineffectual at serving the needs of its clients.

After determining the domain in which you need greater expertise than you have in-house, selecting the strategy consulting firm and finding those experts, you must now set the parameters of the engagement.

Guideline #2: Set the Parameters of the Strategy Consulting Engagement

Level of effort and scope of work — these are the parameters strategy consultants use in pricing their services. You need to help set these parameters. The best way to begin this process is by defining the end product of the engagement, by defining what is "deliverable."

It is important to understand how the engagement fits with the overall strategy of the insurance company. At Prince & Associates LLC, we work through this process with our insurance company clients whenever possible. Questions we always ask our clients are, "How do you plan to use the analysis? research? data?" By understanding where the project fits into the overall thinking of the senior officers, we are able to make certain that we provide the highest level of value. Only in this way can we make sure that all the proper issues are addressed, all the right questions are asked, any and all biases are brought out into the open and all the assumptions make sense.

Inside the management consulting business there are always stories about "runaway projects." These are engagements that take on a life of their own. They are bad for the insurance companies because they usually eat up resources without producing anything of real value for all the time, money and effort expended. Runaway projects are easily avoided by carefully setting and periodically reviewing the parameters of the engagement.

By focusing on the intended results, you have the greatest chance of getting the results you need. You will also be able to optimize the resources you commit to the project.

Guideline #3: Make the Strategy Consulting Engagement a Partnership

Strategy consultants should never think for senior officers. Strategy consultants are brought in because of their unique insurance and financial services industry expertise coupled with their facility with the planning process. Once the project is over, they are going to leave and, therefore, the ultimate responsibility is on the senior officers. Senior officers must be extensively involved.

It should never be a process of the strategy consultants doing *for* the senior officers. It should always be a process of the strategy consultants doing *with* the senior officers. At this level of decision making where strategy consultants are brought in, it must be a partnership between the consultants and the senior officers of the insurance company.

Part of that partnership entails the transfer of expertise from the strategy consultants to the senior officers. Although everything is project specific, insurance companies are best served when they learn from the strategy consultant. Good strategy consultants have a more extensive understanding about their domains of expertise because they are specialists. When they finish the engagement, it is important that all possible information and methods have been transferred to the insurance company.

To facilitate the knowledge exchange, senior officers of the insurance company need to work hand-in-hand with the strategy consultants. They need to be able to freely ask questions and voice their opinions. In the meantime, the strategy consultants need to make the effort to explain the logic they are using. What makes this all work well is good, ongoing, open communication between the senior officers of the insurance company and the strategy consultants.

The Bottom Line

Insurance companies are increasingly using strategy consultants to help them chart a course and capitalize on the dynamic changes impacting the financial services industry. Unfortunately, some of these insurance companies will not benefit from the services of their strategy consultants. In fact, the companies may even be harmed.

In order to obtain great results from your strategy consultants, you will need to stick to three guidelines: (1) carefully select the strategy consulting firm, (2) set the parameters of the strategy consulting engagement, and (3) make the strategy consulting engagement a partnership. This will enable you to maximize the value of working with a strategy consultant.